实用英语
蓝宝书
介词用法大全
BLUE BOOK
OF PRACTICAL PREPOSITIONS

李长庚 ◎编著

 中国纺织出版社有限公司

图书在版编目（CIP）数据

实用英语蓝宝书：介词用法大全 / 李长庚编著. --
北京：中国纺织出版社有限公司，2024.4
ISBN 978-7-5180-8949-9

Ⅰ.①实… Ⅱ.①李… Ⅲ.①英语－介词－研究
Ⅳ.①H314.2

中国版本图书馆CIP数据核字（2021）第202384号

责任编辑：房丽娜　　责任校对：江思飞　　责任印制：储志伟

中国纺织出版社有限公司出版发行
地址：北京市朝阳区百子湾东里A407号楼　邮政编码：100124
销售电话：010—67004422　传真：010—87155801
http://www.c-textilep.com
中国纺织出版社天猫旗舰店
官方微博 http://weibo.com/2119887771
三河市延风印装有限公司印刷　各地新华书店经销
2024年4月第1版第1次印刷
开本：710×1000　1/16　印张：12.75
字数：200千字　定价：49.80元

前 言

英语词汇在1500多年的发展中一直不断增加。最接近完备的词典——《牛津英语词典》(1989年第2版，20卷) 含有60余万单词。然而，据估计，现有的英语词汇在100万以上。

这个拥有庞大词汇的语言中，介词，又称前置词，所占的比例很小。由一个单词构成的简单介词只有100多个，由两个或两个以上单词构成的复杂介词究竟有多少，不可能明确地全部列出，因为从理论上来说，复杂介词可以随时添加到这一语言中。

英语介词是虚词，但同时也是一类重要的功能词。有人指出，英语是一种介词语言。介词的数量是有限的，但其含义极其丰富，用法极其复杂和灵活多变。动词、名词、形容词、副词等与介词搭配，尤其是动词与介词搭配构成无数短语动词。有人曾经指出，学不好介词，就学不好英语。可见，对介词的掌握是学好英语的一个关键。

介词表示两个或两个以上实体之间的空间关系，或两个事件之间的时间关系，或各种其他抽象关系，如手段、原因等 (Cambridge Grammar of English, Carter and McCarthy, 2006, p.462)。

1980年，乔治·莱考夫和马克·约翰逊在其著作《我们赖以生存的隐喻》中指出："在日常生活中隐喻无处不在，我们的语言、思维和行动中都包含了隐喻。"英语中大多数介词都是表示空间的，是人们对空间方位最重要、最直接的语言表达形式之一。隐喻构建了我们领悟、思考的方式和行为。介词表示隐喻意义的例子俯拾皆是，例如：

This question is *beyond* my ken. 这个问题我无法回答。

It would be *beneath* him to do that. 他做那件事未免有失身份。

He is above taking profits *for* himself. 他不屑为自己谋私利。

The children were *beside* themselves with excitement. 孩子们激动得发狂。

When she heard the good news, she felt on *top of* the world. 她听到这个好消息时高兴到了极点。

因此，我们在学习英语时，要特别留心介词的隐喻意义，善于应用，使语言表达简洁生动，富有感染力。

本书共分5个部分：介词分类、介词短语、介词的意义和用法、介词搭配、简单介词的用法。

第1、2、4部分简要叙述了介词分类、介词短语和介词搭配，第3、5两部分是重点。第3部分详细讲解了介词的各种意义和用法。第5部分十分详尽地阐明了118个简单介词的各种用法，用丰富的例句，比较分析了一些介词之间在意义和用法上的差别。

书中如有疏漏或舛误，请读者不吝指正。

编著者

2023 年 8 月

目 录

Ⅰ

1 介词分类

1.1 概述

介词（The Preposition），又称前置词，是一种虚词，用来表示其后面的宾语同句中其他词语之间的关系。介词不能单独担任句子成分，必须连同其宾语构成介词短语，才能在句中担任多种成分。

1.2 介词分类

介词就其构成来说，分为简单介词（Simple Preposition）和复杂介词（Complex Preposition）。

1.2.1 简单介词

简单介词由一个单词构成，常用的有：

aboard, about, above, across, after, against, along, alongside, amid (st), among (st), around, as, at, atop, bar, before, behind, below, beneath, beside, besides, between, beyond, but, by, despite, down, during, except, for, from, in, inside, into, like, mid, midst, near, of, off, on, onto, opposite, outside, over, per, round, since, than, till, through, throughout, to, toward (s), under, underneath, unlike, until, up, upon, via, vice, with, within, without, worth 等。

1.2.2 复杂介词

复杂介词，亦称复合介词（Compound Preposition）或短语介词（Phrasal Preposition）。复杂介词可细分为两个词序列和三个词序列。

（1）两个词序列的复杂介词

所谓两个词序列的复杂介词是指由两个词构成的复杂介词。

①在两个词序列中，第一个词是副词、形容词、分词或连接词；第二个词为简单介词（通常是 for, from, of, to, with）。例如：

according to（根据；依照），ahead of（在…前面），along with（连同…一起），

apart from（除…外，还），as against（与…比较），as for（关于，至于），as from（从…时起），as of（自从；自…起），aside from（不包括；除…以外），as to（关于），as with（与…一样），because of（由于，因为），but for（要不是；如果没有），depending on（取决于，根据），due to（由于；应归于），instead of（代替；而不是；不…而…），irrespective of（不考虑…；不顾…），near to（在…近旁，靠近…），next to（仅次于；与…邻接），on to（到…上；在…上），out of（在…外；从里面；由于；缺乏；在…范围外；用…制成；来自；与…不相称；离开，脱离），owing to（由于，因…之缘故），previous to（在…以前；先于），prior to（在…之前），regardless of（不管，不顾），together with（和；连同；加之），up against（面对；面临），up to（达到；一直到；胜任），upwards of［（数目或价格等）超过］，void of（缺乏；没有）等。

②在两个词序列中，第一个词是简单介词，第二个词也是简单介词。这类复杂介词又称为二重介词。例如：

except for（除…之外，只是），from behind（从…的后面），until after（直到…之后），from among（从…当中），from under（从…下面）等。

（2）三个词序列的复杂介词

①三个词序列的复杂介词中数量最多的一类是由三个词组成的。其构成形式是：

介词1＋名词＋介词2：

at variance with（与…不和，与…不符），by comparison with（和…相比较），by means of（通过；用；借助于），by reason of（由于，因为），by virtue of（依靠，由于），by way of（经由，经过），in addition to（除…之外），in case of（假设，万一），in charge of（照顾；在…掌管之下；由…经管），in common with（和…一样），in comparison with/to（与…比较），in favor of（赞同，有利于），in front of（在…前面），in lieu of（代替），in line with（与…相符合），in place of（代替），in spite of（不管，不顾），in view of（考虑到；由于），with reference to（关于），with regard to（关于），without respect to（不管，不考虑）等。

②三个词序列中还包括这样的复杂介词，其中名词之前有定冠词或不定冠词。例如：

as a result of（作为…的结果；由于），for the sake of（为了），in the light of（按照，根据），on the matter of（关于），with a view to（着眼于；以…为目的；考虑到），with the exception of（除…之外），with the view of（为…的目的）等。

1.2.3　边缘介词

边缘介词（Marginal Preposition）是一类特殊的介词，就是处于边缘状态的介词。边缘介词是由实词向虚词转化而来的，由一个英语单词构成，与动词和形容词关系密切，多用于正式文体或古体语言中。就功能而言，边缘介词在许多方面与完全介词相近，但仍具有其他词类的特点。

边缘介词分为以下几类：

（1）现在分词式的边缘介词：

barring（除…之外；除非），concerning（关于，有关），considering（鉴于；考虑到），counting（包括），excepting（除…之外），excluding（除…之外），failing（如果没有），following（在…之后），including（包括），notwithstanding（尽管，虽然），pending（直到…时；在…以前），regarding（关于），respecting（关于），touching（关于，至于），wanting（缺乏，没有）等。

（2）过去分词式的边缘介词：

given（鉴于；如果；考虑到），gone（迟于，超过），granted（因为，鉴于），past（超过；比…晚）等。

（3）动词原形式的边缘介词：

bar（除…之外），except（除…之外），save（除…之外）等。

（4）形容词式的边缘介词：

worth（值得…的；价值…的），like（像，如同），unlike（不像…，和…不同）等。

（5）连词式的边缘介词：

but（除…以外），except（除了…外；若不是，除非），than（与…相比较）等。

（6）数量词式的边缘介词：

less（减去；不足），minus（减去），plus（加上），times（被乘以…）等。

2　介词短语

2.1　介词短语的构成

介词短语 (Prepositional Phrase) 由介词及其宾语组成。介词宾语可以是名词、代词、数词、形容词、副词、介词短语、不定式、动名词、名词性从句以及复合结构。例如:

Many great scientific discoveries were made more or less *by accident*.

许多重大的科学发现或多或少是出于偶然。(名词)

They were *beside themselves* at the news.

他们听到那消息欣喜若狂。(代词)

She started school *at six*. 她六岁启蒙。(数词)

The police tried *in vain* to break up the protest crowds.

警察企图驱散抗议的人群，但没有成功。(形容词)

Not *until recently* was the scandal of the city official exposed.

直到最近这位市政官员的丑闻才被揭露出来。(时间副词)

It is very cold *in here*. 这里面很冷。(地点副词)

A new moon emerged *from behind the cloud*.

一轮新月从云层后露了出来。(介词短语)

She did nothing *but cry*. 她只是一味地哭。(不带 to 的不定式)

She can do everything *except cook*.

除了做饭外她什么都会。(不带 to 的不定式)

The enemy had no choice but *to lay down* their arms.

敌人别无选择只得放下武器。(带 to 的不定式)

My son seldom comes *except to ask* me for money.

我的儿子除了向我要钱外很少来。(带 to 的不定式)

I have accustomed myself *to working* long hours.

我已习惯于长时间工作。(动名词)

We are puzzled *as to how it happened.*

关于它是如何发生的，我们感到很迷惑。(从句)

She had *no objection to Mary marrying him.*

她不反对玛丽与他结婚。(动名词复合结构)

She came in *with a book in her hand.*

她手里拿着一本书走了进来。(介词 with 引导的复合结构)

2.2　介词短语的语法功能

介词短语在句中作定语、状语、主语补语 (表语)、宾语补语、形容词补语、独立成分、同位语，有时还可作主语。

(1) 作定语

He was a man *with a moustache.* 他是个留小胡子的男人。

(2) 作状语

I agree with you *to some extent.* 我在一定程度上同意你。

(3) 作主语补语 (表语)

All our efforts were *in vain.* 我们所有的努力都白费了。

(4) 作宾语补语

We must not take it *for granted* that the board of the directors will approve the investment plan.

我们决不可想当然地认为董事会一定会批准这个投资计划。

(5) 作形容词补语

Because she's fond *of books* and anxious *for knowledge*, she frequents the library. 因为她喜欢读书，渴求知识，所以经常去图书馆。

(6) 作介词宾语

The sun emerged *from behind the clouds.* 太阳从云层后面露了出来。

(7) 作独立成分

You can buy fruit here—oranges and bananas, *for example.*

你可以在这里买水果，例如柑橘和香蕉。

(8) 作同位语

Please take the chair there, *to the door.* 请把椅子搬到门那儿。

(9) 作主语

Between three and five will suit me. 三点到五点对我合适。

3 介词的意义和用法

3.1 介词的意义

介词含义微妙，用法复杂，可以表示时间、地点、条件、原因、方式、工具、速率、让步、对比、材料、来源、对象、程度、目的、结果、排除、否定，等等。只有在实际应用中勤查字典，反复比较，才能够掌握其各种含义和用法。

3.2 介词的用法

下面分组讨论一些常用介词的用法，至于这些介词的详细用法，参见 5 简单介词的用法详解。

3.2.1 表示时间的介词

表示时间的介词有：about, after, at, before, between, beyond, by, during, for, from, from...to, in, into, inside (of), of, on, over, since, through, throughout, till, to, until, up to, up until 等。

(1) in 表示时间的用法：

① 表示较长时间，如世纪、朝代、时代、年、季节、月及一般 (非特指) 的早、中、晚等。例如：

in the 20th century, *in* the 1950s, *in* 1989, *in* summer, *in* January, *in* the morning/afternoon/evening/night, *in* one's life, *in* one's thirties, *in* the Qing Dynasty 等。

② 用来表示将来时间，in 后面接一段时间时，既可作"在…以后"解，又可作"在…以内"解。若谓语动词表示一时性的行为时，in 作"在…以后"解；若谓语动词表示继续性的行为时，in 作"在…以内"解。例如：

I will come and see you again *in* a week. 我一周后再来看你。(will come and see you again 表示一时性的行为，故译为"一周后")

I will come and see you several times *in* a week. 我一周内将来看你几

次。(will come and see you several times 表示继续的行为, 故译为 "一周内")

比较:
> She will graduate *in* three years.
> 她三年后毕业。(will graduate 是一时的行为)
> She will learn another foreign language *in* three years.
> 她三年内将再学一门外语。
> (will learn another foreign language 是继续行为)

within 要表示 "在···之内", 用介词 within, 避免产生歧义。

比较:
> She will get married *in* a year.
> 她一年后结婚。(get married 是一时的行为)
> She will get married *within* a year.
> 她将在一年内结婚。(within a year 表示一年内)

(2) on 表示具体某一天及其早、中、晚:

on May 1st, *on* Monday, *on* New Year's Day, *on* a cold night in January, *on* a fine morning, *on* Sunday afternoon 等。

注: 如果某日某月在上(下)午之前有 late, early 等修饰语, 介词仍用 in。例如:

> *in* the late afternoon of 1st October 十月一日下午晚些时候

(3) at 表示某一时刻或较短暂的时间, 或泛指圣诞节、复活节等节日:

at 3:20, *at* this time of year, *at* the beginning of..., *at* the end of..., *at* the age of..., *at* Christmas, *at* Easter, *at* Spring Festival, *at* dawn, *at* dusk, *at* evening, *at* night, *at* noon, *at* this moment 等。

注: 在 last, next, this, that, some, every 等词之前一律不用介词。例如:

The market went up a mere point three percent *last week*.

股票市场上周仅上涨了 0.3 个百分点。

Next time I won't allow any excuse from you.

下次我不会再接受你的任何借口。

Where are you going for your holiday *this year*?

今年你打算去哪儿度假?

That year there was a crop failure. 那一年农作物歉收。

He has waited *some time*. 他等了一会儿了。

We meet *every day*. 我们每天见面。

(4) in 和 after 表示"在…之后"的区别："in ＋一段时间"表示将来一段时间以后；"after ＋一段时间"表示过去一段时间以后；"after ＋将来某点时间"表示将来某一时刻以后。例如：

The bus will be here *in* ten minutes. 公共汽车 10 分钟后到这里。

She arrived *after* a week. 她在一星期后到达。

(5) from 和 since 表示"自从…"的区别：from 仅表示什么时候开始，不表示某动作或情况持续多久；since 表示某动作或情况持续至说话时刻，通常与完成时连用。例如：

We work *from* Monday to/till/until/through Friday.

我们从星期一工作到星期五。

I haven't heard from him *since* last year.

我自去年以来未曾收到过他的信。

from 用来表示作为起点的特定时间。例如：

from now on 从今以后

The contract takes effect *from* October 1. 本合同从十月一日起生效。

(6) after 和 behind 表示"在…之后"的区别：after 主要用于表示时间，behind 主要用于表示位置。表示时间时，用于某些固定搭配中。例如：

He will arrive *after* three o'clock. 他将在三点钟以后到达。

The plane was *behind* schedule. 飞机晚点了。

(7) over, through, throughout 均指"经过的全部时间"。例如：

She stayed *over* the holidays. 她一直待到假期结束。

We stayed up *through* the night. 我们熬了一整夜。

It rained *throughout* the night. 雨下了一整夜。

(8) for 和 since 的区别：for 表示动作或状态延续的全部时间长度，表示"长达…"之意；since 用于指从过去特定的某个时刻到说话时为止的一段时间；两者往往用于完成时或完成进行时。例如：

I have been here *for* six years. 我在这里已经 6 年了。

We have not seen each other *since* 1993.

自从 1993 年以来我们彼此未见过面。

(9) by 的用法

① by 表示时间，表示"最迟在…之前"，"到…的时候已经"之意，应注意和它连用的时态。例如：

I was very tired *by* the evening. 我到晚上已经很累了。

② 表示"在…期间"之意，通常连用的名词是 day, night, moonlight, daylight 等，注意名词前通常不用冠词。例如：

He's a waiter *by* day and a comedian *by* night.

他白天做服务员的工作，到了晚上又做喜剧演员。

Our meeting took place *by* moonlight. 我们是在月光下会面的。

She looks older *by* daylight than at night. 她白天比晚上显得老气一些。

（10）during 的用法

① *throughout the course or duration of* 在…的期间。例如：

He left *during* the lecture. 在讲演过程中，他离开了。

② *at some time in* 在…某个时候。例如：

The burglary occurred *during* the night. 这个盗窃案发生在夜间。

③ during 和 in 的区别

　　a. 若表达的是某一段时间，二者可以通用；指具体时间，通常用 in，不用 during。例如：

The old man woke up three times *during/in* the night.

老人夜里醒了三次。

They usually go on holiday *in* July, but last year they went *in* September. 他们通常在七月休假，可是去年是在九月休的假。

　　b. in 和 during 都表示一段时间，凡是能用 in 的地方，一般均可用 during，在这种用法上，during 接近于 in 的意义。例如：

She called on me *during* my absence. 我不在的时候她来拜访我。

You shouldn't call on his wife *in* his absence.

他不在的时候你不应该去拜访他的妻子。

　　c. 当作"在…期间"讲，二者同义，但所表达的时间这一概念，during 表示特指，而 in 则表示泛指。例如：

Where will you be *during* the summer?

夏季你们将去哪儿？（特指今年）

In summer a lot of people go to the seaside.

夏季有许多人到海滨去。(泛指每年)

　　d. 如果表达的是某一时间之后，要用 in，不用 during。例如：

They said the building would be completed *in* a year.

他们说那座楼将在一年后建成。(此句不可用 during)

e. 后面接的名词如果含有时间概念，二者可以通用；否则，通常只能使用 during，而不用 in。例如：

She had some amazing experiences *during/in* her childhood.

她在童年有过一些令人惊奇的经历。(childhood 含有时间概念，用 during 和 in 均可)

He had some amazing experiences *during* his military service.

他在服役期间有过一些惊奇的经历。(service 不含时间概念，不可用 in)

f. during 表示"在…期间"意思时，强调时间的延续，指一个持续的过程，比 in 更强调过程，in 是指在这个过程中。例如：

Many people were killed *in* the war. 许多人死于那场战争。

Albert Einstein suffered a lot *during* the war.

阿尔伯特·爱因斯坦在战争期间受过很多苦难。

g. 此外，在与 visit, stay, meal 等表示事态延续一定时间的名词搭配时，只能用 during, 而不能用 in。例如：

During our visit, we learned how to make colored sculptures.

在参观的过程中，我们了解了如何制作彩塑。

The phone rang *during* the meal. 吃饭时电话铃响了。

(11) beyond 的用法

later than; *after* 迟于；在…之后。例如：

beyond the usual time 比平时晚

Don't stay there *beyond* midnight. 不要过了午夜还留在那儿。

(12) into 的用法

to a point within the limits of a period of time 达到一段时间范围内的某个时候，进入。常与 deep, far, late, well 等副词连用。例如：

The campers sat around the fire deep *into* the night.

露营者坐在火堆周围，一直到深夜。

His thoughts roved far *into* the past. 他沉浸于往事的回忆中。

We carried on the discussion late *into* the night.

我们的讨论一直进行到深夜。

They talked for almost eight hours through dinner and well *into* the night.

他们差不多谈了八个小时，中间吃了一顿晚饭，接着谈到深夜。

(13) of 的用法

① *during or on a specified time* 在某一规定的期间或时间内。例如：

of recent years 在最近这些年中

She has done a lot of reading *of* late. 她最近读了很多书。

② *before; until* 在…之前；直到。与 to 同义，为美式英语，表示"几点差几分"。

five minutes *of* two 差五分到两点

③ of a/an…（时间）表示行为惯常地在此时间发生或进行。例如：

He often goes to the library *of* a Sunday. 星期日他常到图书馆去。

She would read aloud in the classroom *of* a morning.

早晨她往往在教室里高声朗读。

注：上两句中的 of a Sunday 和 of a morning 与 on Sundays 和 in the mornings 同义，但这种表达方式现在已不常见。

(14) through 的用法

① *from the beginning to the end of* 从头到尾，自始至终。例如：

I could not dance, but I sat *through* the party.

我不会跳舞，但我耐着性子待到最后。

② *up to and including* 直到并包括。例如：

The supermarket is open *from* Monday *through* Saturday.

这家超市自星期一一直开到星期六。

注：上句中的 through 是美式英语，英式英语一般用 to 或 up to/till。它所指的时间包括其宾语所表示的时间在内，即包括星期六在内。

(15) to 的用法

① *up till; until* 一直到；直到。常与 from 连用，表示"从…到…为止"。例如：

She works *from* two o'clock *to* ten o'clock. 她从两点工作到十点。

② *before* 在…之前，表示"几点差几分"。例如：

The time is ten *to* five. 现在是五点差十分。

③ 用于某些习惯用语：

to date：到此为止；至今；迄今为止

To date we have received more than five hundred applications.

到此时为止，我们已经收到了五百多份申请书。

to the minute 一分钟不差

My English teacher is punctual *to the minute*.

我的英文老师很守时，一分也不差。

to a/the day 恰好；一天也不差

It's three years *to a day* since we met. 我们整整三年没见面了。

to this day 迄今；直到今天；直到现在

The committee have never heard the whole story *to this day*.

至今委员会还从未听到整个事情的始末。

(16) about, around, round, near, toward (s) 的区别

这五个词均表示 "时间接近于…" 之意。

① about 表示 "大约在…时间"，稍前稍后都可以。例如：

It is *about* six o'clock now. 现在是六点左右。

② 表示 "即将…，正要…"，用于 "be about to ＋不定式" 的句型中。这种句型可以和时间状语从句连用，但不能和表示具体时间的状语连用。例如：

The situation *was about to* boil over. 当时的形势几乎到了紧急关头。

③ around 和 round 的意思与 about 相近，表示 "将近，左右" 之意，around 用于美式英语。例如：

I get up *around* six o'clock. 我差不多六点起床。

They arrived *round* 5 o'clock. 他们是大约五点到的。

He studied *around* the clock for his English exam.

他为了英语考试昼夜不眠地温习。

注：around/round the clock 为习语，意为 "昼夜不停；连续一整天；毫不疲倦地，不松劲地"。例如：

Surgeons are working *round the clock* to save his life.

外科医生们正在日夜工作以抢救他的生命。

④ near 表示 "快要，接近" 之意，只能表示 "稍前"，不能表示 "稍后"。例如：

It's *near* eleven o'clock now. It's time we went to bed.

现在快十一点了，我们该睡了。

⑤ toward (s) 意思和 near 相近，表示"快要，接近"之意。例如：

It began to rain *toward* morning. 快到早晨的时候天开始下雨了。

(17) till/until 和 to 的区别

① till/until 和 to 均可表示"一个阶段的终结"。例如：

The station transmits *from* 6 a.m. *until* midnight.

电台从早晨六点开始播音一直持续到半夜。

② 均可表示距离某一事件发生的时间长度。例如：

It is about half an hour *to/till* supper. 到吃晚餐大约有半个小时。

We plan to postpone the party *to* Saturday evening.

我们打算把派对推迟到星期六晚上。

③ 表示钟点时只能用 to，不能用 till。例如：

It is a quarter *to* ten o'clock. 现在是九点三刻。

④ 与 from 连用时，from...till... 只能用来表示时间，而 from...to... 既可表示时间，又可表示地点和数字。例如：

The museum is open *from* Monday *to* Friday.

博物馆从星期一到星期五对外开放。

We stopped at Paris on our way *from* Rome *to* London.

我们从罗马去伦敦的途中曾在巴黎停留。

⑤ to the end of..., till the end of..., until the end of... 都可以用来表示时间和地点。例如：

I decided to change the meeting *to the end of* the week.

我决定把会议改到这个星期四或星期五。

She remained silent *till the end of* the meeting.

她一直保持沉默，直到会议结束。

Buffett has to answer questions *until the end of* the meeting.

巴菲特一直回答问题，直到会议结束。

⑥ 如果不和 from 连用，除②所说的情况外，一般都用 till，而不用 to。

The rain may last *till* Friday. 可能到星期五都会一直下雨。

(18) as of 表示"自从；自…起"，为书面用语，常用于法律文件。例如：

The new law takes effect *as of* today. 这项新法律从今日起生效。

(19) as from 与 as of 同义。例如：

As from next Monday you can use my office.

从下星期一起，你可以使用我的办公室。

3.2.2 表示地点的介词

表示地点的介词有：aboard, about, above, across, along, alongside, amid(st), among(st), at, atop, before, behind, below, beneath, beside, between, beyond, by, down, from, in, inside, into, near, off, on, onto, opposite, outside, over, through, throughout, to, toward(s), under, underneath, up, upon, via, within, without 等。

地点介词的选择取决于介词补足成分所表示的事物是点还是线，是平面还是立体。地点介词有三种类型，即 at 型、on 型和 in 型。

at 型

at 型地点介词包括 to, at, from 等，常用来表示去向、到达、离开、在或不在某一点。例如：

She goes *to* school at seven every morning. 她每天早晨七点上学。

A red bus stopped *at* the bus stop. 一辆红色公共汽车停在汽车站。

He has been away *from* home for more than 30 years. 他离开家已经三十多年了。

on 型

on 型地点介词包括 along, across, off, on, onto, over, through 等，常用来表示到达、离开、穿过、沿着、在或不在某一条线或某个平面上。例如：

It is a small town *on* the border. 它是一个靠近边界的小镇。

He stepped out of the train *onto* the platform. 他走下火车踏上月台。

We visited an island *off* the coast of southeast last summer.

去年夏天，我们游览了东南沿海的一座岛屿。

He swam *across* the river in the teeth of the storm.

他冒着暴风雨游到了河的对岸。

A beam of moonlight came in *through* the window. 一道月光从窗户射进来。

We went for a walk *along* the shore. 我们沿着海岸散步。

The balcony juts out *over* the street. 阳台延伸到街道上。

in 型

in 型地点介词包括 in, into, out of, through, within 等，常用来表示进入、走出、穿过某个地区、城市或立体物，以及坐落在它们之内或之外。例如：

He has traveled through the country *in* the past 10 years.

在过去十年中他游览了全国。

I have no idea how he got *into* Iraq. 我不知道他是怎样进入伊拉克的。

We waited *in* an adjoining office. 我们在相邻的办公室等候。

Mr Martin was taken *out of* his car at gunpoint.

马丁先生在枪口的威胁之下，从他的小车里被带出。

下面是一些表示地点的常用介词的用法比较：

（1）at, in, on, to

① at 表示在小地方，表示"在…附近；在…旁边"。对于市镇，既可以用 at, 也可以用 in。例如：

He works *at* Haidian. 他在海淀工作。

She has been living *in* Haidian for ten years. 十年来她一直住在海淀。

用 at 仅仅把海淀看作地图上一个地点，不管其内部情况怎样；用 in 则把海淀看作具有一定幅员的具体城镇，居住在其中哪条街道，哪个建筑物，在概念上比较具体。

对于大城市和大城市的街区，通常用 in，如 in Beijing, in Haidian District（海淀区）。但是，当把大城市仅仅看作地图上一点时，就可以用 at。例如：

They stopped first *at* Shanghai, then *at* Tokyo on our way to San Francisco. 他们在去旧金山途中先在上海逗留，然后在东京停留。

同样，arrive at 指到达一个小地方，arrive in 则指到达一个大地方。例如：

We arrived *at* the mountain village late in the afternoon.

我们于下午晚些时候到达那个山村。

He arrived *in* Shanghai at three o'clock in the afternoon.

他于下午三点到达上海。

对于一个建筑物或一组建筑物既可用 at, 也可用 in。用 at 是仅把它看作一个机关，用 in 则是把它看作具体的建筑物。

比较：
> She works *at* the post office.
> 她在邮局工作。
> In the rain she was sheltering *in* the post office.
> 她当时在邮局躲雨。

② at 指句子的主语（说话人）现在不处在的地方，in 则指句子的主语（说话人）现在正处在的地方。例如：

Is there a university *at* that city?

那个城市有大学吗？（问别人所在的城市有无大学）

Is there a university *in* this city? 本市有大学吗？

③ at 用于距离说话人所在地很远的地方（被视为地图上的一点）；in 则用于距离虽很远，但表示在其范围之内。例如：

The 29th Olympic Games met *at* Beijing in 2008.

第二十九届奥运会是 2008 年在北京举行的。

There are many places of historic interests *in* Beijing.

北京有许多名胜古迹。

④ 两个地名连用时，小地名前用 at，放在前面；大地名前用 in，放在后面。例如：

She was born *at* Hangzhou *in* China. 她生于中国杭州。

⑤ on 表示"在…上面，毗邻，接壤"。例如：

There were lots of books *on* his desk. 他书桌上有许多书。

Qingdao is a beautiful city *on* the coast of the Huanghai Sea.

青岛是黄海之滨的一座美丽城市。

⑥ to 表示"在…范围外"，不强调是否接壤；或"到…"。例如：

Nanjing is *to* the west of Shanghai. 南京在上海以西。

It is about 200 kilometers *to* Huangshan from here.

从这里到黄山约 200 公里。

(2) above, over, on

① above 指"在…上方"，不强调是否垂直，与 below 相对。例如：

The bird was flying *above* my head. 那只鸟在我头顶上空飞翔。

② over "在…之上"，指垂直的上方，与 under 相对，但 over 与物体有一定的空间，不直接接触。例如：

There is a bridge *over* the river. 这条河上有一座桥。

③ on "在…之上"，表示在某物体上面并与之接触。例如：

He put his watch *on* the desk. 他把表放在书桌上。

(3) under, below

① under 表示"在…正下方"。例如：

She sat in the shade *under* a tree. 她坐在树荫下。

② below 表示"在…下，不一定在正下方"。例如：

Please write your name *below* the line. 请在这行下面写下你的名字。

(4) in front of, in the front of

① in front of 意为"在…前面"，反义词是 behind（在…的后面）。例如：

A policeman on horseback rode *in front of* the procession.

一名坐在马背上的警察在游行队伍的前面走着。

② in the front of = *in the front part of*, 意思是"在…的前部"，其反义词是 at the back of（在…的后部）。例如：

There is a blackboard *in the front of* our classroom.

我们的教室前部有一块黑板。

比较：
- There was a large hole *in front of* the building.
  大楼的前面有一个大坑。
- There was a large hole *in the front of* the building.
  大楼的前部有一个大坑。

(5) after, behind

① after "在…后面"，表示地点时强调顺序的先后。例如：

Please line up one *after* another. 请按顺序排队。

② behind "在…后面"，表示地点时侧重方向和位置的前后关系。例如：

The student sat *behind* me. 那学生坐在我背后。

3.2.3　表示原因的介词

表示原因的介词有：at, for, from, of, on/upon, through, with, out of, thanks to, for fear of, due to, owing to, because of, on account of 等。

(1) at 多用来表示感情上的原因，常和表示一定感情的词连用。例如：

I'm much pleased *at* your arrival. 你来了我非常高兴。

(2) for "因为"，常表示褒贬、奖惩的原因或内在的、心理的原因。例如：

He didn't answer *for* fear of hurting her feelings. 他没回答是怕伤她的感情。

They sang and danced *for* joy. 他们高兴得又唱又跳。

(3) from 常表示动机或原因，指自然的或直接的原因。例如：

I'm tired *from* work. 我因工作而累了。

The old man died *from* the cold in the winter. 那位老人因为冬天的寒冷而死。

注：die from 表示"因…而死亡"的意思，常指除了疾病、情感等外的原因造成的死亡。其后常跟 pollution, overwork, accident, wound, drinking too much, habit, smoking 等一类表示外部原因或灾祸方面的名词 / 动名词。但有时也可以用来指由于疾病的原因而造成的死亡，只是 die of 比 die from 更常见。例如：

He *died of/from* cancer. 他死于癌症。

(4) through 表示消极的、偶然的、意外的原因和理由。例如：

He lost his job *through* his carelessness. 由于粗心大意，他丢失了工作。

We missed the plane *through* being held up on the motorway.

由于高速公路上交通阻塞，我们误了班机。

(5) of 常用来表示情绪上的原因，因此常与 glad, fond, proud, shamed, tired 等形容词连用。例如：

We're proud *of* being Chinese. 我们因是中国人而感到骄傲。

Don't get tired *of* life; you are still young. 不要对生活感到厌倦；你还年轻。

He is very fond *of* playing basketball. 他非常喜欢打篮球。

We should feel shamed *of* abuse of natural resources.

对滥用自然资源，我们应该感到羞耻。

The beggar died *of* hunger and cold. 那乞丐因饥饿和寒冷而死。

注：die of 常常指由于疾病、年老、情感等原因造成的死亡。其意思为"因…而死"，其后常跟 fever, illness, hunger, thirst, anger, despair, sadness, disappointment, grief 等一类表示内部原因或情感方面的名词。

(6) on/upon（表示为某事物的基础、根据或理由）"由于，因为"，所表示的原因与条件直接相关。例如：

The story is based *on* the fact. 这个故事以事实为依据。

(7) with 多用来表示由外界刺激引起的生理或心理的原因。例如：

Her fingers were red *with* cold. 她的手指冻得发红了。

His face turned red *with* anger. 他气得脸红了。

(8) by "因（某事物）所致；由于；凭借"，通常用来表示由什么方式产生的。例如：

I met her quite *by* chance/accident. 我遇见她完全是偶然的。

He got ill *by* drinking too much yesterday. 昨天由于酒喝得太多，他病了。

(9) in "因为，由于"。 例如：

He cried *in* pain. 他因疼痛而哭了。

还有 due to, owing to, thanks to, because of, on account of 五个短语介词表示 "因为；由于"，但它们在用法上有区别。

(10) because of 用在句首或句子后面，表示直接原因。 例如：

I came late *because of* the heavy rain. 由于交通阻塞我来晚了。

(11) due to "因为；由…引起；由于"，常用作定语或表语。 例如：

Her failure in the speech contest was *due to* her nervousness.

她在演讲比赛中失利，原因是她太紧张了。

(12) owing to = *because of, on account of* "由于；因为"。 例如：

Owing to the rain, the meeting has to be put off. 会议因为有雨而推迟了。

I couldn't attend the meeting *owing to* illness. 我因病不能出席会议。

注： ❶ owing to 在句中作状语，与 because of 的用法有些差别。一般说来，owing to 只引导一个修饰全句的状语，而 because of 引导的状语可修饰句子中的一部分。 例如：

You mustn't punish the child *because of* such a small mistake.

你千万不要因为这样一个小错误而惩罚孩子。

❷ 在现代英语中，due to 可用来引导状语，而 owing to 也可以用来引导表语。 例如：

He was late for school *due to /owing to /because of* the very heavy traffic. 由于交通拥挤他上学迟到了。

because of 通常只用来引导状语，若引导表语，主语通常应为代词。例如：

It is all *because of* what you said. 那完全是因为你说的话。

(13) thanks to "由于，因为；幸亏，多亏"，常位于句首，表示感谢或讽刺意味。 例如：

Thanks to your help, we finished the work a head of time.

多亏你的帮助，我们提前完成了任务。

Thanks to the bad weather, the match had been put off.

由于这倒霉的天气，比赛推迟了。

(14) on account of 与 because of 同义，作 "因为，由于" 解，在句中引导状语。 例如：

On account of the weather, we had to cancel the outing.

因天气原因，我们只得取消郊游。

Traffic suffered *on account of* the snow. 交通因雪受阻。

（15）by reason of 与 because of, on account of 同义。例如：

He was excused *by reason of* his age. 他因为年龄的关系而得到宽恕。

Mr. Miller is a person I hold in reverence *by reason of* his wide courtesy to all people. 米勒先生是我崇敬的人，因为他对谁都不失礼。

（16）out of 表示动机的起因，常译为"由于，出于"。例如：

He did it *out of* concern for everyone. 他这样做是出于对大家的关心。

She did it *out of* jealousy. 她这样做是出于嫉妒。

（17）by/in virtue of = *on account of, by reason of, on the strength of,* "因为，由于；依赖，凭借"。例如：

He has succeeded *by virtue of* industry. 他由于勤奋而获得成功。

（18）in consequence of = *by reason of* "因为，由于"。例如：

In consequence of his bad work, I was forced to dismiss him.

由于他工作表现不好，我只好把他辞退。

（19）on the strength of = *by virtue of, by reason of, on the basis of* "由于，基于"。例如：

I did it *on the strength of* his promise.

我是因为有了他的承诺才做这件事的。

I got the job *on the strength of* your recommendation.

由于您的推荐，我得到了这份工作。

（20）as a result of = *in consequence of* "由于，因…的结果"。例如：

He was late *as a result of* the snow. 由于大雪他迟到了。

Many people are unemployed *as a result of* the economic slump.

很多人因为经济不景气而失业。

3.2.4　表示目的、对象的介词

表示目的、对象的介词有：for, to, at, on, for the purpose of, for the sake of, on behalf of, in honor of, with a view to 等。

（1）for 表示拟定的接收人或目的；to 表示实际的接收人或目的。例如：

I brought the gift *for* my little sister. 我为我的小妹妹带来了礼物。

I gave the gift *to* my little sister. 我把礼物给了我的小妹妹。

(2) for 和 to 都可以引导目的地。for 跟在含有出发或开始意义的动词后，如 leave, set out, start, depart, sail 等；to 跟在含有来往行动意义的动词后，如 go, come, run ,walk, move, fly, drive, ride 等。例如:

They have left *for* Hong Kong. 他们已经离开去香港。

He flew *to* America via Hong Kong. 他经香港飞往美国。

He took out a fire insurance policy *for* his house.

他为自己的房子办理了一份火险保险单。

(3) to (表示目的) 为了；作为。例如:

Having learned that I was in trouble, he came *to* my aid without delay.

得知我陷入困境后，他立即赶来帮助我。

Let us drink *to* the happy pair. 让我们为幸福的一对举杯祝福。

He works hard *to* the end that his family may live in comfort.

为了使家人生活舒适，他勤奋工作。

(4) at = *to or toward the direction or location of, especially for a specific purpose* 向或朝向…某一方向或位置，尤指朝一特定目的。例如:

He rushed *at* me with a knife. 他拿着刀向我冲来。

He shot *at* the bird. 他对准那只鸟射击。

(5) on = *used to indicate actual motion toward, against, or onto* 用于表示实际动作朝向、对着或到…上。例如:

The spotlight fell *on* the actress. 聚光灯把光集中打到女演员身上。

He knocked *on* the door. 他敲门。

(6) on behalf of = *as the agent of; on the part of* 代表；就…而言，为了。例如:

He agreed to testify *on behalf of* the accused man. 他同意为被告作证。

On behalf of my company, I would like to welcome you here.

我代表我们公司欢迎您来这里。

(7) for/with the purpose of 为的是；为了…起见；为了…的目的；以…为目的。

例如:

The teacher paired us off *for the purpose of* the exercise.

为了做练习，老师把我们分成两人一组。

They came here *with the purpose of* making trouble.

他们到这儿来就是为了找麻烦。

（8）for the sake of 为了；为…起见。例如：

He is going to live by the coast *for the sake of* his health.

他为了自己的健康，打算到海滨地区居住。

（9）with a view to 为了，目的在于。例如：

He studied English hard *with a view to* mastering it quickly.

他为了尽快精通英语而努力学习。

We bought a jeep *with a view to* visiting my parents in the countryside.

我们买了一辆吉普车，为的是去乡下探望我的父母。

（10）in honor of 为纪念；为向…表示敬意；为…庆祝。例如：

A dinner is to be given *in honor of* the new president. 将为新校长举行晚宴。

He dedicates the book to the prestigious scholar *in honor of* his achievements in literature.

他把此书献给这位令人尊敬的教授，以向他在文学方面的成就致敬。

3.2.5　表示条件的介词

表示条件的介词有：but for, except for, in, in case of, in the absence of, in the event of, under, with, without 等。其中，有的介词只能用于虚拟条件句，如 but for；有的既可以用于真实条件句，也可以用于虚拟条件句。

（1）but for = *if it were not for*; *without* "要不是；如果没有；没有"，只用于虚拟条件句。例如：

But for the rain we would have had a nice holiday.

要不是因为下雨，我们的假日一定过得很惬意。

But for music, life would be dull. 要不是有音乐，人生会很无聊。

（2）except for = *but for*; *if it were not for* "要不是；如果没有"。例如：

Except for you, I should be dead now. 如果没有你，我现在可能死了。

She would leave her husband *except for* the children.

要不是因为这些孩子，她就会离开她的丈夫。

（3）in = *in a situation or condition* 在某种情形或条件下，可用于真实条件句或虚拟条件句。例如：

The instrument can be used *in* the circumstance of no power supply.

该仪表可适用于野外没有电力电源供电的场合。

I would have done the same *in* that position.

如果我处在那个位置，我同样会做的。

(4) in case of = *if there should happen to be* "如果发生"。例如：

Press this button *in case of* fire. 遇火灾时按下此钮。

Many people are at a loss as to what to do *in case of* a real fire.

一旦真的发生火灾，许多人就不知所措，不知道该干什么好了。

(5) in the absence of = *without*, 意为 "缺乏…时，当…不在时"。例如：

In the absence of friction belted machinery would not be used.

没有摩擦力，皮带传动的机器就无法使用。

This chemical reaction would not take place *in the absence of* a special catalyst. 如果没有特殊的催化剂，就不可能发生这种化学反应。

(6) in the event of = *if it should happen* "如果发生；万一发生"。例如：

Call the police *in the event of* an emergency.

万一发生紧急情况就打电话给警察。

In the event of rain, the party will be held indoors.

万一下雨，聚会就在室内举行。

(7) under "在…情况下"。例如：

I cannot help doing so *under* these circumstances.

在这样的情况下我不得不这样做。

We might have done better in our research *under* more favorable conditions.

如果条件更有利，我们的研究工作也许会做得更好。

(8) with 用于条件句，意为 "如果有，有"。例如：

With a little assistance, Alexander will succeed.

只需要一点儿帮助，亚历山大就会成功。

Now we can reduce the production costs *with* the help of the computer.

现在有这台电脑帮忙，我们就能降低生产成本了。

(9) without 用于条件句，意为 "如果没有，要没有"。例如：

Without health, happiness is impossible. 没有健康就不可能有幸福。

3.2.6　表示结果的介词

表示结果的介词有：in, into, to 等。

(1) in = *to or at a situation or condition of* 达到或处于某种状态或情形。例如：

The whole comedy can be split *in* two parts. 整个喜剧可以分为两部分。

I am *in* debt again this month. 我这个月又入不敷出了。

All their efforts ended *in* failure. 他们的一切努力都以失败而告终。

Until recently, the company was *in* the red. 最近该公司出现了赤字。

They succeeded *in* climbing the mountain. 他们成功地登上了山。

In conclusion, I'd like to say how much I've enjoyed staying here.

最后我想要说，我在这里过得有多愉快。

In the final analysis the will of the people is irresistible.

归根到底，人民的意志是不可抗拒的。

（2）into

① *to the condition, state, or form of* 达到…的条件、状态或形式。常与
change, develop, grow, transform, turn 等表示变化的动词搭配。例如：

Intense cold turns water *into* ice. 严寒使水变成了冰。

She developed *into* a beautiful woman. 她长成了一位漂亮的女人。

A steam engine transforms heat *into* power. 蒸汽机将热能转变成动力。

② 表示"把…译成、分成、换成"，"使…成为，进入某种状态、突然
发生"等。与这类动词搭配的有：alter, burst, connect, convert, divide,
exchange, explode, put, slice, translate 等。例如：

I require to alter some British sterling *into* Renminbi.

我需要把一部分英镑换成人民币。

The trees burst *into* bloom. 那些树木突然开花了。

The entire hall burst *into* applause. 全场爆发出一阵掌声。

The students are divided *into* several small groups to talk about the
subject. 学生们分为几个小组讨论那个主题。

Some stars explode *into* spectacular supernovas.

有些星星会爆炸，形成壮观的超新星。

She put the story *into* English. 她将这个故事译成了英语。

Peel the radish and slice it *into* 1cm thick each.

把萝卜去皮，切成每块 1 厘米厚。

Winners translate dreams *into* reality. Losers translate reality *into* dreams.

成功者把梦想变为现实，失败者把现实变为梦想。

③ 表示某种特殊原因所造成的结果，常与某些动词，如 allure（引诱），
argue（说服），beguile（欺骗；诱骗），bribe（贿赂），bully（欺侮），cajole（哄

骗，勾引），cheat（欺骗），coax（欺骗，哄骗），coerce（强迫；威迫），conduct（引导），deceive（欺骗），dupe（欺骗，愚弄），entrap（诱陷），fool（愚弄，欺骗），force（强迫），frighten（吓唬，恐吓），humbug（欺骗），persuade（说服，劝说），pressure（迫使），provoke（驱使），reason（劝说），scare（吓唬），shock（使惊恐），stare（凝视，瞪视），sting（促使），talk（说服），tempt（勾引，引诱，怂恿），terrify（威胁），threaten（恐吓，威胁），trepan（诱入圈套，欺骗），trick（欺骗），wile（欺骗，诱骗）等搭配，构成 ... sb. into (doing) sth. 这一有用句型。例如：

They allured her *into* a snare. 他们诱她落入圈套。

My younger sister thinks she can argue Father *into* increasing her monthly pocket money. 我妹妹认为，她能极力说服父亲增加她每个月的零用钱。

She stared him *into* silence. 她把他盯得不吭声了。

You cannot talk her *into* marriage. 你不能说服她结婚。

You can't trick me *into* sympathizing with you. 你骗取不了我的同情。

(3) to

① *reaching as far as* 达到…。例如：

The ocean water was clear all the way *to* the bottom.

海水从上面一直到海底都是清澈的。

The tree planted by the magician quickly grew *to* a monstrous height.

魔术师种下的树很快就长得极其高大。

② *to the extent or degree of* 到…的范围或程度。例如：

She loved him *to* distraction. 她如此爱他，以至于心神不宁。

③ with the resultant condition of 以…为最后结果。例如：

The seedling was frozen *to* death. 幼苗被冻死了。

The town came *to* life after sunrise. 日出之后，这个市镇变得充满生气。

His emotional language reduced many of the audience *to* tears.

他满怀感情的话语使许多观众流下眼泪。

To our delight, our football team won.

令我们高兴的是，我们的足球队赢了。

The old lady tore the letter *to* pieces. 老太太把信撕成碎片。

(4) out of = *used to indicate result*，用来表示结果。例如：

She tried to talk him *out of* his plan. 她试图说服他放弃他的计划。

He talked his wife *out of* buying a new car. 他说服妻子不买新车。

He cheated me *out of* my money. 他骗了我的钱。

3.2.7　表示方式、方法、手段的介词

表示方式、方法和手段的介词有：after, as, by, in, on, like, through, with, without, by means of 等。

（1）after = *in the style of or in imitation of* 以⋯的风格，模仿⋯。例如：

This fable was written *after* the manner of *Aesop*.

这则寓言是仿照《伊索寓言》写成的。

The study shows that fewer and fewer schools are being named *after* people.

这项研究显示越来越少的学校用人名来命名。

（2）as

　　① in the role, capacity, or function of 充当⋯角色、身份或功能。例如：

　　I want to work *as* a porter in a hotel. 我想在旅馆里当一名搬运工。

比较：
- I worked *as* a slave. (I am a slave).
  我以奴隶身份工作。（我是奴隶。）
- I worked *like* a slave.
  我像奴隶一样地工作。

　　② *in a manner similar to*; *the same as* 以⋯相似的方式；和⋯一样。例如：

　　On this issue they thought *as* one. 在这个问题上，他们意见一致。

　　Many people use education *as* a stepping stone to a better life.

　　许多人将教育作为通往更美好生活的跳板。

（3）by

　　① *through the agency, means or instruments of* 由于⋯之作用、方法或工具；借着；由；被。例如：

　　The streets are lighted *by* electricity. 街道用电照明。

　　She makes a living *by* writing. 她靠写作谋生。

　　② *indicating path or means of travel, transport, conveyance* 表示旅行、运输之路线、工具或方法。例如：

　　I'd rather they came *by* land than *by* water.

　　我宁愿他们从陆路来，而不从水路来。

　　He told me the news *by* telephone. 他电话告诉我这消息。（不用冠词）

The quickest means of travel is *by* plane.

最快的旅行途径是乘飞机。(不用冠词)

比较:
He arrived at the airport *in* a brand-new car.
他乘坐一辆崭新的小车到达机场。(不可用 by)
We will go there *on* a launch.
我们将乘汽艇到那儿去。(不可用 by)

比较:
The man was killed *by* lightning.
那男子被被电击死。
(雷电是一种作用，而非工具，不能用 with。)
The rat was killed *by* Tom with a stick.
那只老鼠被汤姆用棍子打死。

(4) in

① *after the style or form of* 以某种风格或形式。例如:

a poem *in* iambic pentameter 以五音步抑扬格写成的诗

He behaved *in* a very strange fashion. 他的举止很奇怪。

② *indicating the method of expression, the medium, means, material, etc.* 表示表达的方法、媒介、工具、材料等。例如:

He sent a message *in* code. 他用密码发送了一份讯息。

That letter was written *in* pencil. 那封信是用铅笔写的。

Henry called for the waiter *in* a loud voice. 亨利大声叫那个服务员。

The statue was cast *in* bronze. 这座塑像是用青铜铸成的。

Are you paying *in* cash or by credit card?

您是现金支付还是用信用卡付账?

Cloth is often measured *in* meters. 布常用米为丈量单位。

I bought the washing machine *in* instalments.

我用分期付款的方式购买了那台洗衣机。

(5) on

① *used to indicate a means of conveyance* 用来表示运输方式。例如:

Six people were travelling in a compartment *on* a train.

有六个人搭乘火车旅行，他们坐在同一车厢内。

He stowed away *on* a ship to Britain. 他偷乘轮船到英国。

They met by chance *on* a plane. 他们在飞机上不期而遇。

② *used to indicate the agent or agency of a specified action* 用于表示某一特定行为的作用。例如：

He cut his fingers *on* the broken glass. 他被碎玻璃割破了手指。

They talked *on* the telephone. 他们在电话中交谈。

Some boys smoke *on* the sly. 有些男孩子偷偷地吸烟。

③ *used to indicate availability by means of* 用以表示用…方式获取。例如：

Doctors should be *on* call at any hour. 医生应随时都能出诊。

I have my own word processor and printer at home, so that everything I need is *on* tap. 我家有自己的文字处理机和打印机，因此我需要什么就随时可以取用。

(6) like = *in the typical manner of; in the same way as* 以…的典型方式；以…同样方式；像。例如：

He works *like* a beaver. 他像河狸一样地工作。

I wish I could sing *like* her. 我希望能像她那样唱歌。

(7) through = *by the means or agency of* 通过…途径或作用。例如：

She became rich *through* hard work. 她通过辛勤劳动而致富。

They were opposed to change *through* violence. 他们反对通过暴力变革。

Rocks are worn smooth *through* the agency of water.
岩石由于水的作用而变得光滑。

Through two years of efforts, a negotiation attended by all those concerned was finally arranged. 经过两年的努力，最终安排好了所有相关人员都参加的会谈。

(8) with

① *in the manner of* 以…的方式。例如：

He made us laugh *with* his jokes. 他以他的笑话引我们发笑。

The girls jumped up and down and waved their arms *with* abandon.
那些女孩子尽情地跳上跳下，挥舞着手臂。

② *by the means or agency of* 用；通过…的方式或作用。例如：

He opened the door *with* his key. 他用钥匙开了门。

We eat food *with* a fork. 我们用叉子吃东西。

(9) without = *in the absence of* 没有，无。例如：

He went away *without* taking leave. 他不辞而别。

Everybody can come to this school, *without* respect to class, race, or sex.

不论阶级，种族，性别，人人都可进这所学校读书。

(10) by means of: 通过；用；借助于。例如:

Thoughts are expressed *by means of* words. 思想是用（通过）言语表达的。

He succeeded *by means of* perseverance. 凭着坚忍不拔的毅力，他成功了。

My garden communicates with the garden next door *by means of* a gate.

我的花园与隔壁的花园有门相通。

(11) by the agency of: 靠…的力量；通过…的作用。例如:

They are transacting business *by the agency of* a broker.

他们正在通过中间人做交易。

Iron is melted *by the agency of* heat. 铁由于热能的作用被融化。

I've got this job *by the agency of* my teacher.

借助于老师之力我得到了这份工作。

(12) in terms of

① *as measured or indicated by* 用…衡量或表示。例如:

The cost was calculated *in terms of* the current price.

成本是以现在的价格计算的。

② *in relation to; with reference to* 根据，按照；就…而言。例如:

The cost was calculated *in terms of* the current price.

成本是以现在的价格计算的。

Indeed, reserves of gas already stand at 87 percent of oil reserves *in terms of* energy content. 的确如此，就能源存量而言，天然气的蕴藏量已经达到石油的87% 了。

3.2.8 表示比较、对比、对照、区别的介词

表示比较、对比、对照、区别的介词有: above, against, before, behind, below, beneath, beside, beyond, by, for, from, in, over, past, than, to, under, with, as against, as compared with, compared to, compared with, in comparison with, in contrast to/ with, in excess of 等。

(1) above = *superior to in rank, position, or number; greater than* 在级别、地位或数量上高于、优于；比…更大。例如:

Mary is two grades *above* me. 玛莉比我高两个年级。

Principles should be put *above* expediency. 原则应高于权宜。

A miser loves gold *above* his life. 守财奴爱财胜过生命。

(2) against = *in contrast or comparison with the setting or background of* 对照；对比；与…的布景或背景相对比。例如：

a majority of 10 *against* 3 10 比 3 的多数票

The picture looks better *against* the light wall.

这幅画挂在浅色的墙上显得更美。

They were dancing *against* the background of a rising sun.

他们在一轮冉冉升起的红日的映衬下跳着舞。

(3) before

① *superior in a position to* 地位高于。例如：

The prince is *before* his brother in the line of succession.

在王位继承权上，这个王子优于他兄弟。

He always put the interests of others *before* his own.

他总把他人的利益放在第一位。

② *rather than; sooner than* 宁可…也不愿；与其…宁可。例如：

He will die *before* he submits. 他宁死不屈。

I will die *before* I will betray my country. 我宁可死也不会背叛我的国家。

(4) behind

① *below the standard level; in or into an inferior position* 处于标准水平以下；处于或陷入下等地位。例如：

I am *behind* him in English. 我英语不如他。

We are all *behind* him in maths. 我们数学都不如他。

② *hidden or concealed by* 被…隐藏或掩盖。例如：

Treachery lurked *behind* his smooth manners.

他圆滑姿态的后面潜伏着奸计。

There must be something *behind* the plan. 这项计划后面必有隐情。

(5) below

① *lower than* 低于。例如：

A captain in the army ranks *below* a captain in the Navy.

陆军上尉其军衔低于海军上校。

② *unsuitable to the rank or dignity of* 有失身份，对社会阶层或尊严来说不合适。例如：

He considered the job *below* his dignity. 他认为这种工作有失身份。

Some husbands still think it *below* their dignity to do the shopping.
有些做丈夫的至今仍然认为让他们去买东西是件丢面子的事。

注：句中 below 与 beneath 同义，可互换。

（6）beneath

① *lower than, as in rank or station* 低于…，如在等级或地位上低于。例如：

I could never stoop to such conduct as that; I should consider it *beneath*
me. 我绝不会降低人格去干那种事，我认为我不屑于此。

Snobs are usually contemptuous of people they feel to be *beneath* them.
势利者通常瞧不起他们认为地位在他们之下的人。

② *unworthy of; unbefitting* 不值得；有损于。例如：

It was *beneath* me to beg. 不值得我去乞求。

Such an accusation is *beneath* contempt. 这种谴责是不值一顾的。

（7）beside

① *in comparison with* 与…相比较。例如：

You're quite tall *beside* your brother. 与你兄弟相比，你是相当高的。

Beside yours our achievement counts for little.
与你们的成就比较起来，我们的算不了什么。

② 用于某些习惯用法。

　　a. *beside the point* 离题。例如：

　　Please don't say anything *beside the point* in your speech.
　　请不要在发言时说任何与主题无关的话。

　　What you say may be true, but in this case it is completely *beside the
　　point*. 你所说的可能是真的，但在这个事件上根本就离题了。

　　b. *beside oneself = in a state of extreme excitement or agitation* 发狂；处
　　于异常兴奋或激动状态。例如：

　　The children were *beside themselves* with excitement.
　　孩子们激动得发狂。

　　The children were fairly *beside themselves* with joy as they caught sight
　　of their parents. 孩子们见到父母简直欣喜若狂。

(8) beyond

① *to a degree that is past the understanding, reach, or scope of* 达到超出理解、限度、范围之上的程度。例如：

His ideas are quite *beyond* my ken. 我很不理解他的想法。

The slum area was sordid and filthy *beyond* belief.

该贫民区之污秽肮脏简直令人难以置信。

② *to a degree or amount greater than* 达到大于…的程度或数量。例如：

The good they have done for me is *beyond* measure.

他们对我所做的好事简直无可估量。

The level of inflation has gone *beyond* 6%. 通货膨胀率已经超过了 6%。

(9) by = *used to indicate the difference in the amount or number of, usually used after comparatives* 用于表示数目或数量相差，常用于比较级之后。例如：

He is taller than I *by* a head. 他比我高一头。

His horse won *by* a nose. 他的马以一鼻之差取胜。

I was only late *by* five minutes. 我只迟到了五分钟。

(10) for = *considering the nature or usual character of; in view of* 就…的性质或一般特征而言；鉴于，表示某种含蓄比较。例如：

He is tall *for* his age. 就他的年龄而言，他是个高个子。

It's quite warm *for* January. 就一月而言，天气相当暖和了。

(11) from

① *used to indicate differentiation* 用以表示区别，常与 contradistinguish, differentiate, discriminate, distinguish, know, tell 等动词连用。例如：

We have to learn to contradistinguish one thing *from* another.

我们必须学会用对比的方法来区别两个事物。

Can you differentiate one variety *from* the other?

你能将这两个品种区别开来吗？

Studying literature enables us to discriminate good books *from* bad ones.

研读文学能使我们从坏书中辨别出好书。

Speeches distinguish human beings *from* animals.

语言把人类和动物区别开来。

We should know right *from* wrong. 我们应辨别是非。

② 与某些表示"不同"意义的形容词连用，如 different, distinct, diverse, divergent 等。例如：

The English language is different *from* any other language.

英语同其他任何语言都有所不同。

There is an atmosphere of peace and calm in the country, quite different *from* the atmosphere of a big city.

在乡间有一种和平宁静的气氛，和大城市的气氛截然不同。

注：如果表示"在…不同"，要用介词 in。例如：

The two boys are different *in* their tastes.

这两个男孩的爱好是相异的。

Gold is distinct *from* iron in property. 金在性质上不同于铁。

The word is now used in a sense diverse *from* the original meaning.

在某种意义上说，此词现在的含义与最初的含义完全不同。

Second, his unique translation method makes his renderings divergent *from* "faithfulness". 其次是他的翻译方法背离了忠实性原则。

(12) in = *used to indicate the ratio or proportion* 用于表示比率或比例。例如：

a slope/gradient of one *in* five 五分之一的斜坡 / 坡度

He paid his creditors 25p *in* the pound.

他向他的债权人按每镑二十五便士偿还。

Not one *in* ten of the boys could spell well.

这些男孩中拼写正确的不到十分之一。

(13) over

① *indicating superiority un rank, authority, etc.* 表示在等级、军阶、权威等方面处于优势；高于。例如：

Over 200 people were present at the wedding ceremony.

超过二百人出席了婚礼。

Our new product gives us an advantage *over* our competitors in terms of both quality and cost.

我们的新产品在品质与价格方面都胜过竞争对手。

② *in preference to* 优先于。例如：

I favor his ideas *over* all the others. 我偏爱他的想法。

You can select happiness *over* tears. 你可以选择快乐而非痛苦。

(14) past

① *beyond the power, scope, extent, or influence of* 超出…的权力、范围、程度或影响力。例如：

It is *past* my power. 这是我力所不及的。

I was *past* caring now, so I ordered coffee for myself and an ice-cream and coffee for her. 那时我已经不在乎什么了，就给自己点了咖啡，给她点了咖啡和一份冰淇淋。

② *beyond in development or appropriateness* 在进展或适宜程度方面超出。例如：

The old man is *past* work. 那老头已干不了活了。

The writer's *past* eighty but he's still writing industriously.

这位作家已年过八旬，但他仍在勤奋地写作。

③ *beyond the number or amount of* 在数目或数量方面超过。例如：

He is *past* fifty. 他年过五十了。

The child couldn't count *past* 20. 这个孩子的年龄不可能超过20岁。

(15) than = *in comparison with* 与…比较。例如：

His way of living is different *than* ours. 他的生活方式跟我们的不同。

She was different *than* any other girls he had ever known.

她跟他所认识过的女孩都不同。

注：❶ different from/to 多用于英式英语，different than 为美式英语。例如：

Their schools are *different from* our schools in China.

他们的学校与我们中国的学校不一样。

He said that life in the USA was very *different to* life in China.

他说美国的生活与中国的生活很不一样。

You look *different than* before. 你看上去跟从前不同了。

❷ different 后面未紧接介词时可用 than。例如：

比较：
How *different* life today is *than* what it was 30 years ago!
今天的生活与三十年前相比是多么不同啊！
Life today is *different from* the life 30 years ago.
今天的生活不同于三十年前的生活。
（from 在 different 后）

（16）to

① *used to indicate comparison, ratio, preference, reference* 用来表示比较、比率、偏爱、优先选择、参照。例如:

The score was 9 *to* 5. 得分是 9 比 5。

He's quite rich now, compared *to* what he used to be.

同他过去比起来，他现在很富有了。

It's nothing *to* what it might be. 比起可能的结局，这算不了什么。

I prefer tea *to* coffee. 我喜欢茶胜过咖啡。

The picture is true *to* life. 这幅画画得逼真。

② for each 每一 = *when comparing two amounts; when quoting a rate* 比较两个数量或谈及比率时。例如:

petrol consumption of 30 miles *to* the pound

每加仑汽油可行驶 30 英里

a tax of 10p *to* the pound 每镑抽 10 便士的税

（17）under

① *less than; smaller than; lower than in degree, amount, age, time, price, etc.* 表示在程度、量值、年龄、时间、价格等低于…；在…以下；未满；不足；少于；小于。例如:

My shirt cost *under* twenty dollars. 我的衬衫价钱不到 20 美元。

I can't go into that bar. I am *under* age.

我不能进那个酒吧，我还没成年呢。

People who are either *under* age or over age may not join the army.

年龄不到或者超龄的人都不得参军。

② *inferior to in status or rank* 地位或等级低于… 例如:

They work *under* a kind leader. 他们在一个和蔼的领导手下工作。

There were nine officers *under* me at the headquarters.

在总部有九个军官职位低于我。

（18）as against 与…比较。例如:

The production of various stereo recorders has been increased four times *as against* 1977. 各种立体声录音机的产量比 1977 年增长了三倍。

The business done this month amounts to twenty thousand dollars *as against* nine thousand dollars last month.

这个月生意的总额为 20000 美元，上个月为 9000 美元。

(19) as compared with 与…相比。例如：

As compared with others, he is no ordinary professor.

与其他人相比，他是一位非凡的教授。

Our price is reasonable *as compared with* that in the international market.

我们的价格和国际市场的价格相比还是合理的。

(20) compared to 与…相比。例如：

Compared to investing, savings also means avoiding risk.

与投资相比，储蓄也意味着规避风险。

Compared to ours their house is a palace.

他们的房子和我们的相比简直就是宫殿。

(21) compared with 和…比较。例如：

Compared with a quite ordinary star, like the sun, the earth is small indeed.

与一个很普通的恒星如太阳相比较，地球的确很小。

Imports in the first three months have increased by 10 percent *compared with* the corresponding period last year.

第一季度的进口额与去年同期相比增长了百分之十。

(22) in comparison with 和…比较起来。例如：

In comparison with other students, Mike is more diligent.

和其他学生相比，迈克更加勤勉一些。

Living in the country is cheap *in comparison with* big cities.

与大都市相比之下，在乡下生活较便宜。

(23) in contrast to/with 与…形成对比；与…相比。例如：

In contrast with their system, ours seems very old-fashioned.

我们的制度与他们的相比，显得过于守旧了。

In contrast to traditional costing systems, the activity-based costing system has many advantages.

与传统成本计算制度相比较，作业成本计算制度具有许多优点。

(24) in excess of: greater than; more than 大于；多于；超过。例如：

Our school has a student number *in excess of* 800.

我们学校的学生人数超过了八百人。

I never do anything *in excess of* my ability.

我从不做超出自己能力范围的事。

3.2.9 表示赞成、反对的介词

表示"赞成、反对"的介词有: for, by, behind, with, against, in favor of, in opposition to, in agreement with, in sympathy with 等。

(1) for = *in favor of*; *in support of* 对…赞成; 对…支持、拥护; 主张。 例如:

They are all *for* him. 他们都拥护他。

Were they *for* or against the proposal? 他们支持这项议案还是反对呢?

I made my position clear that I would never agree to vote *for* him.

我非常清楚地表明了自己的立场: 我决不会同意投他的票。

We stand *for* a peaceful settlement of the international dispute.

我们主张和平解决这一国际争端。

(2) by = *at or to the side of*; beside 意为"在…近旁; 在…旁边; 向…旁边", 与动词 stand 等连用, 表示"站在…旁边", 引申为"支持、拥护"。 例如:

True friends are those who will stand *by* you.

忠实的朋友是那些会支持你的人。

(3) behind = *in a position of support*; *at the back of* 处于支持的位置; 支持; 在…的后面; 做…的后盾。 例如:

The leaders have the army *behind* them. 那些领袖有军队作为后盾。

Don't be afraid. We're all *behind* you! 不用怕, 我们大家都支持你。

(4) with

① *in support of*; *on the side of* 支持, 赞同; 在…的一边。 例如:

I hear what you are saying and I am *with* you.

我知道你要说什么, 我同意你的观点。

He turned around and voted *with* the Whigs.

他改变了宗旨, 投了辉格党人的票。

② *of the same opinion or belief as* 与…一致; 与…有相同的观点或信仰。
例如:

He is *with* us on that issue. 在那个议题上他和我们观点一致。

Are you *with* me or against me in this matter?

对于这件事, 你是赞成还是反对我?

③ *in opposition to*; *against* 反对；对抗。例如：

wrestling *with* an opponent 与对手摔跤

Politicians don't much like it either, because it means a fight *with* business.
政治家们也不太喜欢，因为这表示要跟企业作对。

(5) against = *in hostile opposition or resistance to*; *opposed to* 处于敌对状况或
与…对抗；反对。例如：

No one is *against* this proposal. 没有人反对这个提议。

Virtue will prevail *against* evil. 美德必将战胜邪恶。

(6) in favor of 支持，赞同；有利于。例如：

Not everyone was *in favor of* this bill. 并不是每个人都拥护这个法案。

I would be *in favor of* making it illegal to smoke while driving.
我会支持立法禁止驾车时吸烟。

The judge decided *in favor of* the plaintiff. 法官作出了有利于原告的裁决。

(7) in agreement with 符合…；同意；和…一致。例如：

He nodded *in agreement with* me. 他点头表示同意我的意见。

We are *in agreement with* their decision on that point.
在那一点上我们同意他们的决定。

(8) in opposition to 反对。例如：

He spoke at the meeting *in opposition to* the unpractical plan.
他在会上反对那项不切实际的计划。

Those who are *in opposition to* the bill put up your hand.
反对该议案的人举手。

(9) in sympathy with 赞成…；同情…。例如：

I am *in sympathy with* your suggestion. 我赞同你的建议。

We are *in sympathy with* his plan and arrangement.
我们赞同他的计划和安排。

3.2.10　表示让步的介词

表示让步的介词有：after all, despite, for all, in defiance of, in spite of, in (the) face of, in the teeth of, irrespective of, no amount of, notwithstanding, regardless of, with all 等。

(1) after all 尽管。例如：

After all, a better opportunity might yet present itself.

毕竟，一个更好的机遇也许已经出现了。

After all my advice, he insisted on going.

尽管我一再劝阻，他仍然坚持要去。

(2) despite 不管；不顾；即使。例如：

He came to the meeting *despite* his illness.

尽管生病，他还是来参加了会议。

Despite the bad weather we enjoyed our holiday immensely.

即使天气不好，我们的假期仍过得非常愉快。

(3) for all 尽管。例如：

He never stopped trying *for all* his failures.

尽管他失败了，但他从没放弃努力。

For all its merits, the alloy does not measure up to the requirements.

尽管这合金有许多优点，还是不符合要求。

(4) in defiance of 无视，不服从，不顾。例如：

He climbed the ladder *in defiance of* the warning.

他无视警告爬上了那架梯子。

Bob jumped into the river *in defiance of* the icy water.

鲍勃不顾冰冷的水跳入了河中。

(5) in spite of 尽管，不顾。例如：

In spite of great efforts, they failed to carry their plans through.

尽管作出了巨大努力，他们还是没能完成计划。

He persisted in carrying on the experiment *in spite of* all kinds of setbacks.

尽管遇到很多挫折，他仍坚持做实验。

(6) in(the)face of 不顾。例如：

He succeeded *in face of* great danger. 尽管危险重重，他还是成功了。

In the face of all evidence they made as if they had had no hand in it.

尽管证据俱在，他们却装作好像没有插手这事。

(7) in the teeth of 不顾。例如：

The new policy was adopted *in the teeth of* fierce criticism.

那项新政策尽管受到强烈抨击却硬是被采用了。

He maintained his stand *in the teeth of* public opinion.

他不顾公众舆论的反对而坚持自己的立场。

(8) irrespective of 不考虑…, 不顾…。例如:

It must be done, *irrespective of* cost. 不论花费多少，这件事一定要做。

The law applies to everyone *irrespective of* race, religion or color.

这项法律适用于所有人，不管其种族、宗教或肤色。

(9) no amount of 怎么 (再多) 也…不; 尽管。例如:

No amount of persuasion on the part of the nurse could restrain him from rising. 无论护士怎样劝说，都阻止不了他要起床。

No amount of money can compensate for my father's death.

我父亲的死不论多少钱也不能弥补。

(10) notwithstanding 虽然，尽管。例如:

Notwithstanding all difficulties, we managed to push the matter through.

尽管困难重重，我们还是把事情完成了。

Notwithstanding any other agreements, we will make a new contract with the firm. 尽管有其他的协议，我们仍将与这家公司签订一份新合同。

(11) regardless of 不管，不顾。例如:

She is determined to do it *regardless of* all consequences.

她不顾一切后果，决心这样做。

Regardless of expense, we must take every measure to save the old man's life. 不管费用多少，我们必须采取一切措施抢救这位老人的生命。

(12) with all 尽管。例如:

With all his wealth, he is not happy. 尽管他很有钱，但是他并不幸福。

With all her experience, she could not get a job.

尽管她很有经验，她还是找不到工作。

3.2.11 表示原料的介词

表示原料的介词有: from, in, of, on, out of, with 等。

(1) from *used to indicate the material, etc. used in a process, the material being changed as a result* 表示原材料等在制造过程中有所改变。例如:

Wine is made *from* grapes. 葡萄酒是用葡萄酿成的。

Steel is made *from* iron. 钢是由铁炼成的。

（2）in 意为"以 / 用…原料、材料"，指制成品材料的色调或特性。例如：

We have furniture of this design *in* oak and *in* walnut.

我们有这种设计式样的橡木和胡桃木家具。

He chiseled out a statue *in* a block of marble.

他在一块大理石上凿出一尊雕像。

It is impolite to write a letter *in* red ink. 用红墨水写信是不礼貌的。

（3）of *indicate material or substance*; *composed of or made from* 表示材料或质料；由…组成或由…制成。例如：

a dress *of* silk 绸衣

a table *of* wood 木桌

His house was built *of* brick. 他的房子是用砖砌成的。

These appliances are made *of* stainless steel. 这些器具是用不锈钢制成的。

There is an ornament made *of* shells on the wall.

墙上有一个贝壳做成的装饰品。

注：❶ 东西制成后，材料仍看得出来的，用 of。东西制成后，成品与原料在形状和性质方面都有所改变，原料已看不出原来的样子，用 from。

❷ consist, make up, build up, form, compose, comprise 等常与 of 搭配，表示"由…组成或构成的"，其中 consist of 只能用于主动语态。例如：

All bodies *consist of* molecules and atoms.

一切物质都是由分子和原子构成的。

Life *is made up of* little things. 人生是由琐碎的事物构成的。

Japan *is formed of* four large islands. 日本是由四个大岛构成的。

Water *is composed of* hydrogen and oxygen. 水由氢和氧组成。

Everything *is built up of* atoms. 万物都是由原子构成的。

His lunch *was comprised of* many different meats and vegetables.

他的午餐包含了不同的肉类和蔬菜。

About two-thirds of trading volumes *were comprised of* government securities. 大约三分之二的交易额来自政府证券。

（4）out of *from or with a material* "以 / 用…材料"，与 of 同义。例如：

Many items in daily use are made *out of* plastic.

有很多日常生活用品是塑料制的。

The house was made *out of* stone. 这座房子是用石头建造的。

（5）with 表示制成产品的一种成分，或者"以…技术工艺"制成。例如：

A fruitcake is made *with* fruit. 果糕是用水果做的。

Traditional moon cakes are usually made *with* bean paste.

传统的月饼是用豆馅做的。

注：with 是指制造或建造某种东西的材料之一，而不是全部，如上句，豆馅只是制成月饼的成分之一。of 则指制造或建造某种东西的全部材料或所有的成分。

This set of glass curio was made *with* the latest technology.

这套玻璃古玩是用最新工艺制作的。

3.2.12　表示状态、情况的介词

表示地点的介词都可以用来表示状态或情况。这些表示状态或情况的介词在5简单介词的用法部分都有所涉及，下面简要谈谈表示状态和情况的几个介词。

（1）at

① *in a state or condition of* 在某一状态或状况下。例如：

Our hometown is *at* its best in May. 我们的家乡五月最美。

The escaped prisoner is still *at* large. 那个逃犯仍然逍遥法外。

② *occupied with* "忙于，从事于"。例如：

What are you *at*? 你在干什么？

During the Second World War, Germany was *at* war with almost all the countries in the world. 第二次世界大战期间，德国几乎同世界上所有的国家处于交战状态。

（2）in

① *to or at a situation or condition of* 达到或处于某种状态或情形中。例如：

You know how happy you are when you are *in* love.

当你沉浸在爱中，你就会懂得你是多么幸福。

His extravagance explains why he is always *in* debt.

他挥霍无度，难怪总欠债。

② *having the activity, occupation, or function of* 有…活动、职业或作用。例如:

He has serious aspirations to a career *in* politics. 他有从政的雄心壮志。

The advertising campaign is still *in* preparation. 广告宣传攻势仍在准备中。

③ *during the act or process of* 在…行动或过程中。例如:

The party was *in* full swing when we arrived.

我们到达时恰值聚会的高潮。

We sent them off *in* high spirits. 我们兴高采烈地给他们送别。

(3) on

① *used to indicate the state or process of* 用来表示…的状态或过程。例如:

His assistant appeared to be *on* leave. 他的助手显然是在休假。

The orchestra is currently *on* tour in Germany.

该管弦乐团目前正在德国巡回演出。

② *used to indicate addition or repetition* 用来表示增加或重复。例如:

Their company suffered loss *on* loss in business last year.

他们公司去年在生意上接二连三地亏本。

Heaps on heaps of rubbish on the land make the environment unhealthy.

陆地上成堆成堆的垃圾使环境变得对健康有害。

③ *used to indicate the purpose of* 用来表示…的意图。例如:

Do you travel to China *on* business often? 你经常来中国做生意吗?

I've come *on* a special errand. 我是专程来办一件差事的。

(4) about

① *in the act or process of* 在…行动或进程中。例如:

While you're *about* it, please clean your room.

趁你正在清理, 请打扫一下你的房间。

② *occupied with* 从事于, 忙于。例如:

What are you *about*? 你在干什么?

(5) into

① *to the activity or occupation of* 从事…的活动或职业。例如:

Robson now hopes to go *into* "something banking-related" after university.

罗布森现在希望大学毕业后能从事"与银行业相关的"职业。

After graduation from Cambridge John launched *into* politics.

剑桥大学毕业后约翰就投身了政界。

② *to the condition, state, or form of* 变为…的状况、状态或形式。例如：

She dropped the vase and it broke *into* pieces.

她一失手，花瓶掉下碎成碎片了。

The ugly caterpillar will change *into* a beautiful butterfly.

丑陋的毛毛虫会变成美丽的蝴蝶。

When she saw me she burst *into* tears. 她一看见我就放声大哭。

(6) below

① *lower than* 在…以下。例如：

The temperature is *below* zero. 温度在零度以下。

He was *below* her in intelligence. 他的智力比她低。

② *unsuitable to the rank or dignity of* 有失身份，对社会阶层或尊严来说不合适。例如：

Such petty behavior is *below* me. 如此卑劣的行为有失我的身份。

(7) from

① *used to indicate a specified state or condition as a starting point* 用来表示作为起点的特定状态或情况，常与介词 into 或 to 搭配。例如：

The sky slowly changed *from* blue *to* red. 天空慢慢由蓝色变为红色。

His temper is going *from* bad *to* worse these days.

这些日子，他的脾气越变越坏。

There are different ways of changing energy *from* one *into* another.

有各种不同的方法把能量从一种形式变成另一种形式。

② *used to indicate* a change *in state or condition* 用来表示状态或情况的变化或转变。例如：

He awoke *from* a dream in the night. 夜里他从梦中醒来。

The earth is awakening *from* the long winter sleep.

大地正在从漫长的冬眠中苏醒过来。

(8) under

① *used to indicate "inferior to in status or rank"* 用来表示"地位或等级低于…"。例如：

Mr Gray is *under* me in the company. 在公司格雷先生的职位低于我。

He is in our department and works *under* me.

他在我们部门，是我的下属。

② *used to indicate a state or condition in which sth. or sb. is* 用来表示某事或某人所处的状态或情况。例如：

Now inflation seems to be *under* control.

现在通货膨胀似乎在控制之中。

I will pay nothing *under* compulsion. 在强迫之下我分文也不愿支付。

Food and clothing will not get cheaper *under* existing conditions.

在目前的条件下，食品和衣服不会变得便宜些。

A defeated country usually signs a treaty of peace *under* compulsion.

战败国通常被迫签订和约。

(9) in the case of 就…而言，在…情况下。例如：

In the case of Europe the issue is complicated by market interventions and politics. 就欧洲而言，由于市场干预和政治因素，这个问题很复杂。

In the case of a limited company, the secretary or a director should sign.

对股份有限公司而言，公司秘书或董事应签名。

注：in case of 作"万一，如果发生"解。例如：

Break the circuit first *in case of* fire. 如遇火警，先断开电路。

I have kept a reserve fund *in case of* accidents.

我已筹备了一笔准备基金以防不测。

(10) in course of 在…进行中。例如：

The highway is *in course of* construction. 这条高速公路正在施工中。

Everything is *in course of* continuous movement, change, and development in the world. 世界上的一切事物都处在不断运动、变化和发展中。

注：in the course of = *during the course of*，意为"在…期间；在…过程中"。例如：

My heart beat thick *in the course of* the interview.

在面试过程中我的心跳得厉害。

(11) in (the) face of 意为"面临；不管"。例如：

They showed courage *in the face of* danger.

面对危险他们表现出了勇气。

You should keep calm even *in face of* danger.

即使面临危险，你也应当保持镇静。

（12）out of = *in a state or position away from the expected or usual* 表示"处于出乎意料的或不寻常的状态或状况"。例如：

More airlines will go *out of* business, especially as the price of oil is rising again. 将有更多航空公司停止运营，尤其是在油价再度走高的情况下。

The squirrel ran up a tree and got *out of* my reach.

松鼠跑到树上去了，我逮不着。

When rates of inflation get *out of* hand, financial markets often break down.

当通货膨胀失去控制时，金融市场就常常会崩溃。

The lorry ran down the hill *out of* control. 卡车失去控制直往山下冲去。

3.2.13　表示量度的介词

表示量度的介词有：at, by, for, in, off, to 等。

（1）at

　① 表示速度、价格等，意为"以…，按…"。例如：

　　Eggs are sold *at* 95 cents a dozen here. 这里的鸡蛋每打 95 美分。

　　The airliner flies *at* about 900 kilometers a hour.

　　这架班机以每小时 900 公里的速度飞行。

　② 用于表示温度、角度、利率。例如：

　　Water boils *at* 100 degree centigrade. 水在 100 摄氏度时达到沸点。

　　The tow lines inclined to one another *at* an angle of 60.

　　两条线成 60 度角互相倾斜。

　　The commercial bank lends money *at* the interest rate of 6.5 percent.

　　这家商业银行以 6.5% 的利率贷款。

　③ 用于表示比率、比例。例如：

　　Party A and Party B shall share profits, risks and losses *at* the ratio of each contribution to the registered capital.

　　甲乙双方应根据在注册资本中所占的比例来分享利润、风险和损失。

　　Individual housing loans are *at* the lowest proportion of the first payment 20%. 个人住房贷款最低首付款比例仍为 20%。

　　注：at 用于表示比率、比例，但不是绝对的，有时可用其他介词。

　　例如：

　　Our product outsells theirs *by a ratio of* two to one.

我们的产品比他们的畅销，销售量为他们的二倍。

Men outnumber women here *in the ratio of* three to one.

这里男女比例是三比一。

The number of strikes increased *in direct ratio to* the rise in the cost of living. 罢工次数与生活费用的上涨成（正）比例地增加。

Transport by air has the highest cost but it is fast *with* the lowest ratio of loss and damage. 空运是所有运输里面成本最高的方式，但是同时也是速度最快、破损率最低的方式。

This door is narrow *in proportion to* its height.

这扇门就其高度的比例而言窄了些。

(2) by

① by 表示单位，意为"以…计"，其后通常接表示计量单位的单数名词，而且名词前要用定冠词。例如：

They are paid *by* the day/month. 他们所得报酬按天 / 月计。

Milk is sold *by* the pint, butter *by* the pound, and eggs *by* the dozen.

牛奶按品脱卖，黄油按磅卖，蛋类按打卖。

② 有时也接抽象名词，通常不用冠词。例如：

We sell them *by* wholesale, not *by* retail. 我们是做批发销售的，不零售。

They were charging us *by* volume rather than *by* weight.

他们是按体积而不是按重量向我们收费。

③ 也可以接复数形式的数词。例如：

And they sat down in ranks, *by* hundreds, and *by* fifties.

于是众人就一排一排地坐下，有一百一排的，有五十一排的。

The leaflets are to be distributed *by* hundreds of high school students.

这些传单将由数以百计的中学生发放。

④ 用来表示"根据…标准；按…计算"。例如：

Our crime rate remains low *by* any standard.

以任何标准来看，我们的犯罪率都一直处于低水平。

By this measure it's been a weak economy all along — and now it's falling off a cliff.

按照这个标准看，经济长期疲软——现在则正从悬崖向下坠。

Between 1974 and 1997, the number of overseas visitors expanded *by*

27%. 在 1974 年和 1997 年之间，外国游客数量增加了 27%。

He lives in a room 5m *by* 4m. 他住在一间长五米宽四米的房间里。

(3) for

used to indicate equivalence or equality 用于表示等值、相等关系，"以⋯为价钱、代价；付出"。例如：

I bought the ticket *for* five pounds. 我花了五英镑买了那张票。

We bought apples and pears, paying two to three dollars *for* a bushel.
我们买了苹果和梨，一蒲式耳装的水果大约为 2 到 3 美元。

(4) in

① *used to indicate the second and larger term of a ratio or proportion* 用于表示次要的和较大的比例或比率。例如：

It is said that one *in* ten people has reading problems.
据说十分之一的人存在阅读障碍问题。

②(表示数量、程度、比例) 按⋯；以⋯。例如：

It was a murder *in* the second degree. 这是二级谋杀。

Please pack the books *in* tens. 请将这些书十本一包地包好。

Would you mind giving me some dollars *in* tens and in fives?
您能给我一些十美元和五美元的钞票吗？

America has fallen to the ninth *in* the proportion of young people with a
college degree. 美国年轻人中有大学学历的比例已经下降到了第九名。

Are you paid *in* proportion to the number of hours you work?
你是按工时数付酬吗？

(5) off

① *not up to the usual standard of* 没达到通常水准的。例如：

He seems to be *off* his game. 他看上去比赛状态不佳。

② *lower than; subtracted from* 低于⋯；从⋯扣除。例如：

He is three years *off* forty. 他差三岁就到四十了。

Can you take $10 *off* the price? 你能把价格减少 10 美元吗？

He offered to take 10% *off* the price.
他表示愿意原价减去百分之十。

We cannot take anything *off* the price. 我们不能再减价了。

(6) to

表示数量与单位，意为"每…"。例如：

12 *to* the dozen 每打 12 个

500 persons *to* the square kilometer 每平方公里 500 人

3.2.14　表示交换、代替和当作的介词

表示交换或替代的介词有：for, as, in place of, instead of, in lieu of, in the name of, in substitution for, on behalf of, in exchange for 等。

(1) for

① *on behalf of*; *in place of* "代表…；代替…"。例如：

Red is *for* danger. 红色代表危险。

Plastics are often used as a substitute *for* steel. 塑料常用来做钢的代替品。

② *in exchange for* "交换…"。例如：

My deskmate wanted to trade his pen *for* my book.

我的同桌想用他的钢笔换我这本书。

We cannot use money to barter *for* life. 我们无法用钱财换取生命。

Today's exchange rate is 6.3 yuan *for* a dollar.

今天的汇率是一美元兑换 6.3 元人民币。

③ *as being* "当作…"。例如：

Do you take me *for* a fool? 你当我是傻瓜吗？

What do you want *for* a present? 你要什么样的东西作礼物？

Nowadays, commuters take traffic jams *for* granted.

时下的通勤者认为交通堵塞是理所当然的。

He is to stand *for* York at the next election.

他将在下届选举中做约克郡选区的候选人。

(2) as

in the role, capacity, or function of "以…角色、身份或功能"。例如：

The trusty SIM card can also act *as* a debit and credit card.

可信的用户识别卡也可以作为借记卡和信用卡来使用。

These philosophical views serve *as* a guide in life.

这些哲学观点可以作为处世指南。

She left school three years ago and has been working *as* a nurse ever since.

她三年前毕业，从那时起便一直当护士。

The forest will act *as* a defense against desert dust.

森林能起防御沙漠灰沙的作用。

He will act *as* guide and liaison. 他将充当向导和联络员。

We must appoint him to act *as* secretary. 我们必须任命他当秘书。

注：as 用来表示"以…角色、身份或作用"，当名词被抽象化时，可不用
不定冠词 a/an ，如上两句。

(3) in place of 代替；用…而不用…。例如：

Use olive oil *in place of* butter. 用橄榄油代替黄油。

Credit cards are now widely used *in place of* cash or checks.

信用卡现在已被广泛地用来取代现金或支票。

注：in place of 意为"代替"，in the place of 意为"在…的地方"；take the
place of 意为"代替"，定冠词不可省略。例如：

In the place of dreams, hell is paradise. 在有理想的地方，地狱就是天堂。

Electric trains have *taken the place of* steam trains in many countries.

在许多国家，电气火车已经代替了蒸汽火车。

(4) instead of（用…）代替…。例如：

To save money, I purchased a used car *instead of* a new one.

为了省钱，我没买新车，而是买了辆二手的。

(5) in lieu of 代，替代。例如：

I accept a check *in lieu of* cash. 我接受支票代替现金。

(6) in the name of 以…的名义；代表。例如：

I greet you *in the name of* the President. 我代表总统前来迎接您。

You will all fall upon him *in the name of* law and order.

你们都以法律和秩序的名义向他猛扑过去。

(7) in substitution for 以替代。例如：

We eat plenty of vegetables *in substitution for* fruit.

我们吃很多蔬菜以替代水果。

We use saccharin *in substitution for* sugar. 我们用糖精代替糖。

(8) on behalf of 为了…的利益；代表…。例如：

The man agreed to testify *on behalf of* the accused man.

该男子同意为被告作证。

(9) in exchange for 交换。例如:

He gave me an apple *in exchange for* a cake. 他给我一个苹果，换一块蛋糕。

3.2.15 表示分离、距离、清除的介词

(1) from

① *used to show how far apart two places are* 用以表示两地间的距离、间隔。例如:

100 meters *from* the scene of the accident. 距事故现场 100 米。

He lives three miles away *from* here. 他住在距离这里三英里的地方。

② *used to indicate separation, removal, prevention, escape, avoidance, deprivation* 用以表示分离、除去、阻止、逃避、避免、剥夺等。例如:

The party was ousted *from* power after eighteen years.

十八年后该党被赶下台。

He shielded his eyes *from* the sun. 他把手放在眼前遮住太阳光。

③ 与介词 from 搭配的常用动词有:

absolve sb. from (赦免某人的…), abstain from (戒…，节制…), cease from doing sth. (停止做某事), conceal sth. from sb. (对某人隐瞒…), defend sb. from (保护某人以免…), deliver sb. from (从…解救某人), differ from sth. (和…有区别、差别；和…不同), discharge sb. from (免除某人的…；允许某人离开…), discourage sb. from doing sth. (劝阻某人做…), dismiss sb. from (开除、解除某人的…), dismiss sth. from (从…消除…), dissent from (不同意…；和某人意见不一致), distinguish sth. from sth. (识别…和…), divide…from… (把…从…隔离开), eliminate sth. from (从…把…排除掉、排出), ensure sb. from sth. (保护某人免受…), escape from (从…逃跑、逃脱；从…漏出、流出), exclude sb. from (拒绝某人加入、进入…), excuse sb. from (给某人免去…), expel sb. from (从…驱逐、开除某人), guarantee sb. from (确保某人免于…), hide sth. from sb. (对某人隐瞒…), hinder sb. from doing sth. (阻止、阻碍某人做…), inhibit sb. from doing sth. (禁止某人做…), isolate…from (把…从…隔离开), keep sth. from sb. (对某人隐瞒…), keep sb. from doing sth. (阻止、抑制…做…), know…from (区分…和…), liberate … from (把…从…

解放 / 释放出来；解除），obstruct sb. from doing sth.（阻挠某人做…），oust sb. from（把某人从…驱逐 / 撵走 / 赶走），part from sb.（同某人分手、告别），prevent sb. from doing sth.（阻止某人做…），prohibit sb. from doing sth.（禁止、阻止某人做…），protect…from（保护…以免…），refrain from doing sth.（忍住、抑制住做…），relieve sb. from（消除某人的…），remove sb. from（从…把某人开除；撤某人的职），rescue sb. from（从…处 / 状况下营救某人），resign from（辞去…职务），restrain sb. from doing sth.（制止、遏制…做…），retire from（从…退职、引退、隐居等），retreat from（放弃…；从…退出），save sb. from（把某人从…救过来），secure sb. from（保护某人以免…），separate…from…（把…和…分开、分离），shelter sb. from（掩护某人以免…），shield sb. from…（保护某人免受…），stop sb. from doing sth.（阻止某人做…），tear sth. away from（从…夺走…），tell…from（把…和…区别开），wander from（离开正道；离题），withdraw…from（把…从…撤回），withhold from doing sth.（忍住不做…），withhold sth. from sb.（对某人隐瞒…）

(2) of

① *indicating separation in space or time* 表示空间或时间的间隔。例如：

a quarter *of* three 差一刻钟三点

within a year *of* his death 他死后一年内

The Chaohu Lake is about 64 kilometers south *of* Hefei.

巢湖在合肥以南约 64 公里处。

② *indicating relief, deprivation, riddance* 表示"解除、剥夺、免除"。

与 of 搭配的常用动词有：bereave（剥夺，使失去），cheat（骗，骗取），cleanse（使清洁，清洗），clear（扫除，清除），cure（治愈），deprive（剥夺，使丧失），disarm（解除…的武装），divest（剥夺；脱去；剥掉），ease（减轻；放松），heal（治愈），lighten（减轻），plunder（掠夺，抢劫），purge（清洗；整肃；清除），relieve（减轻；免除；解除），rid（使摆脱；解除，免除；清除），rob（抢夺，抢掠，剥夺），strip（脱，剥；剥去；除掉）等。例如：

He was bereaved *of* his wife last year. 去年他痛失爱妻。

When not fighting they spend their time in deep meditation to cleanse themselves *of* their sins.

当没有战斗的时候，他们就会入定禅思以清除他们内心的罪恶。

They cleared the street *of* snow. 他们扫除了街上的积雪。

The purpose of that resolution was to disarm Iraq *of* its weapons of mass destruction. 决议的目的是解除伊拉克的大规模毁灭性武器。

The police divested the pretended officer *of* his stolen uniform.

警察剥掉了那个冒牌军官偷来的制服。

Try to purge your spirit *of* hatred. 尽量洗净你灵魂中的仇恨。

The wind stripped the trees *of* all their leaves. 风吹落了所有的树叶。

③ 与某些形容词搭配，如 bare, empty, free, scant, short, shy, sparing, void 等，表示"无，没有，缺乏"等含义。例如：

The room is bare *of* furniture. 这个房间什么家具都没有。

At night these busy streets during the day become empty *of* traffic.

夜里，这些白天繁忙的街道空无行人车辆。

The village school is scanty *of* textbooks. 这乡村学校奇缺教材。

The country is short *of* skilled labor. 这个国家缺乏技术工人。

This product is void *of* defects. 这件产品没有缺陷。

(3) off

① *down from; away or relieved from* 从…下来；离开，从…解脱开。例如：

Leaves fall *off* the trees in the autumn. 秋天，树叶纷纷从树上落下来。

Tears rolled *off* her cheeks. 泪水从她双颊滚下来。

A policeman does not wear his uniform when *off* duty.

不值勤时警察不穿制服。

② *from* 从…。例如：

She bummed a dollar *off* me. 她向我讨了一美元。

He borrowed a pound *off* me. 他借我一英镑。

A week's work sweated 6 pounds *off* him.

一个星期的劳动使他减轻了六磅体重。

We are as a whole, why do you separate *off* us from each other?

我们是一个整体，为什么要把我们分开？

③ *at some distance (in space or time) from* 离…一些 (空间、时间) 距离。

例如：

The house stands miles *off* the main road. 那所房子离大路好几英里远。

She is three years *off* thirty. 再过三年她就满三十岁了。

④ *feeling averse to*; *not taking or indulging in* 对…感到讨厌；嫌恶；不吃；不饮；不抽；不沉溺于。例如：

I'm *off* food. 我没有食欲。

She's *off* drugs. 她不再服药了。

3.2.16 表示结合、归属、附属的介词

（1）with

① *in the company of*; *accompanying* 和…一起；在…陪伴下；随同。例如：

Did you go *with* her? 你跟她一起去的吗？

She likes talking *with* her friends. 她喜欢和她的朋友聊天。

With the advent of the rockets, the Space Age began.

随着火箭的出现，太空时代开始了。

People should not identify wealth *with* happiness.

人们不能把金钱和幸福等同起来。

It is necessary to integrate theory *with* practice. 理论联系实际是必要的。

② *in the charge or keeping of* 负责，照料。例如：

She left the cat *with* the neighbors. 她把猫托邻居照顾。

I will leave a message *with* his secretary. 我会给他的秘书留言。

③ *in support of*; *on the side of* 支持，赞同。例如：

I'm *with* anyone who wants to help the homeless.

我支持任何想帮助无家可归的人。

My mother did not sympathize *with* my proposal.

我母亲并不赞同我的建议。

④ *in accord with*; *of the same opinion or belief as* 和…一致；符合…；与…有相同观点或信仰。例如：

Onion does not agree *with* me. 洋葱不适合我的胃口。

He is *with* us on that issue. 在那个问题上他和我们观点一致。

（2）to

① *used to indicate appropriation or possession* 用于表示归属或占有。例如：

the key *to* the lock 这把锁的钥匙

He looked for the top *to* the jar. 他找到了这个罐子的盖子。

a private secretary *to* the minister 部长的私人秘书

Such a man is an honor *to* his country. 这样的人是他国家的光荣。

She affiliated her child *to* Smith. 她判定孩子是史密斯的。

② *as an accompaniment or a complement of*; *in accord with* 作为…的伴随或补充；与…一致；适合。例如：

We danced *to* the disco music. 我们伴随着迪斯科音乐跳舞。

He'll sing *to* the accompaniment of the piano. 他将在钢琴的伴奏下唱歌。

Such fiscal constraints, however, do not apply *to* new regulations.
然而，这样的财政限制不适用新规定。

His father takes a liking *to* coin collecting. 他的父亲喜欢收集货币。

(3) along with 连同…一起；随同…一起。例如：

She was sworn in, *along with* other eleven jurors.

她与其他十一位陪审员一起宣誓就职。

I can't go *along with* your view. 我不能赞同你的观点。

(4) alongside with 与…一起；除…以外。例如：

Brand concept emerges *alongside with* the business competition, and plays a more and more important role in nowadays corporate value.

品牌伴随商业竞争而出现，在企业价值中品牌所占的比重越来越大。

The reform of education should be further carried out *alongside with* the promotion of quality education, thus improving the sense of creation and the ability to deal with actual things.

深化教育改革，着力推进素质教育，重视培养人的创新意识和实践能力，提高人才培养质量。

(5) together with 和，连同。例如：

These new facts, *together with* the other evidence, prove the prisoner's innocence. 这些新的事实连同其他证据已证明该囚犯无罪。

He sent me the book, *together with* a letter. 他把书寄给我，还附上了一封信。

(6) in combination with 与…联/结合；与…协力；与…共谋。例如：

The company is developing a new product *in combination with* several research institutes. 该公司正在联合几家研究所开发一种新产品。

(7) in company with 和…一起。例如：

She came *in company with* a group of girls. 她同一群女孩子一起来的。

I went to London *in company with* my husband. 我是和丈夫一起去伦敦的。

(8) in conjunction with 和…一道，结合。例如：

We are working *in conjunction with* the police. 我们与警方配合进行工作。

The novel should be read *in conjunction with* the author's biography.

这本小说应该和作者传记一起读。

(9) in collaboration with 与…合作／合著；与…勾结。例如：

They worked *in collaboration with* each other. 他们相互合作。

Right now I am writing a book *in collaboration with* one of my colleagues.

我现在正与我的一位同事合写一本书。

(10) in harness with 同…合作。例如：

He had to work *in harness with* them. 他不得不同他们一起工作。

(11) in league with 与…联合；与…勾结。例如：

She was *in league with* her mother to embarrass me.

她和她母亲联合起来叫我下不了台。

The police suspected that the bank clerk was *in league with* the rubbers.

警察怀疑银行职员与强盗有勾结。

(12) in tandem with 同…串联，同…合作。例如：

During the 2007 financial crisis, corporate profits fell *in tandem with* empleyment. 2007 年的金融危机中，企业利润与就业同步下降。

As the yuan sinks *in tandem with* the dollar, China is able to keep its export prices low and price out any competition. 随着人民币与美元一道走软，中国能够保持低的出口价格，以价格优势赢得任何竞争。

3.2.17　表示关于的介词

表示关于的介词有：about, of, on, with, as comcerns for, as to, in the matter of, in connection with, in/with reference to, as regards, in/with regard to, in respect of/to, in terms of, concerning, regarding, respecting, touching 等。

(1) about

① *concerning, regarding*; *in connection with* 关于…；与…有关。常与表示听、说、读、写、思考、同意等义的动词搭配。例如：

It was great to hear *about* your new job.

听说你找到新工作了，这太好了。

Can we speak *about* the plan for the holidays?

我们谈谈假期的打算好吗？

What are you talking *about*? 你们在谈论什么？

I read *about* the film in the newspaper.

我在报上读到过有关这电影的文章。

I happened to know *about* him. 我正好了解一些他的情况。

He will have lots to write *about*. 他到时候会有很多事情去写。

I don't agree *about* the book. 我不同意对这本书的评价。

She always thinks *about* her children first. 她总是首先考虑到自己的孩子。

注: about 所表示的关系，比 of 要详细些。把 of 加在 agree, hear, know, read, speak, talk, think, write 等动词后面，表示关于某人或某事物的存在；把 about 置于这些动词后面，则表示关于某人或某事物的详情。例如:

I don't know Tom but I know *of* him. 我不认识汤姆，但我听说过他。

I know *about* him. 我了解他。

② *in reference to*; *concerned with* 关于…；与…相关。与某些形容词搭配，构成（be）+ adj. + about 结构。例如:

He is careless *about* his appearance. 他不关心自己的仪表。

I'm very uneasy *about* the interview. 我对这次面试感到很不安。

She's very *particular about* what she wears. 她对衣着很讲究。

注: 与 about 搭配的常用形容词: angry, anxious, careful, careless, certain, curious, disappointed, easy, envious, excited, glad, happy, mad, nervous, particular, sad, serious, sure, uneasy, worried 等。

(2) of

① *with reference to*; *about* 关于。例如:

They think highly *of* him. 他们很敬重他。

Your boss speaks very highly *of* your work.

你的老板对你的工作称颂备至。

This is a long story *of* adventure. 这是一个很长的冒险故事。

We may talk *of* beautiful things, but beauty itself is abstract.

我们尽可谈论美的事物，然而美本身却是抽象的。

注：与 of 搭配的常用动词：admit, allow, approve, despair, disapprove, dispose, dream, permit, smell, taste, tell, treat 等。例如：

The facts *allow of* no other explanation. 这些事实不允许有其他解释。

I *approve of* your choice. 我赞成你的抉择。

They *despaired of* winning the game. 他们不抱比赛得胜的希望。

I can *dispose of* all his arguments easily.

我能轻而易举地驳倒他所有的论点。

I *dream of* exploring Antarctica one day. 我梦想有一天能在南极洲探险。

The situation does not *permit of* any delay. 情况不允许有任何耽搁。

The house *smells of* paint. 这房屋有油漆的气味。

His hands *tell of* heavy labor. 他的双手显示他干的是粗活。

The second volume of the series *treats of* the social changes between the wars. 丛书的第二卷论述了两次大战之间的社会变化。

② *in respect to* 就…来说。与某些形容词搭配，构成（be）+ adj. +结构。例如：

He is *slow of* speech. 他讲话很慢。

The dog is *shy of* strangers. 这狗害怕生人。

注：与 of 搭配的常用形容词：afraid, ashamed, aware, capable, careful, certain, fond, free, full, glad, nervous, proud, short, shy, sick, sure, tired, worthy 等。

（3）on

① *concerning*; *about* 关于；论及。例如：

a book *on* grammar 一本语法书（专著）

The doctor gave us a talk *on* health.

这位医生就健康方面的问题给我们做了一个报告。

Professor Li will give us a lecture *on* international affairs.

李教授将要给我们做关于国际形势的演讲。（正式演讲）

注：如前所述，of 仅仅表示有关某人某事，而并不涉及其详情；about 表示较为详细地谈论某人某事，把某人某事作为谈话的对象；在这三个表示"关于"的介词中，on 最为正式，表示专论某人某事，把某人某事作为主题。

② 与某些动词、形容词、过去分词连用，表示决心、决定、坚持做某事。例如：

She is *bent on* buying a new house. 她一心想买一套新住房。

I have determined *on/upon* going to the countryside after graduation. 我已决定毕业后到农村去。

He *insisted on* immediate payment. 他坚持要求对方立即付款。

Sally is *keen on* music, amount other things, she plays the violet three times a week.

萨利十分喜爱音乐，除了其他活动以外，她每周演奏三次小提琴。

He was *set on* becoming a doctor. 他决心当个医生。

(4) with = *in regard to* 关于，对于；就…而言。例如：

We are pleased *with* her decision. 她这样决定，我们很高兴。

Will you be quite frank *with* me about this matter?

在这个问题上你能不能真正地跟我说实话？

It is day *with* us while it is night *with* them.

对于我们此时是白天，而对于他们则是夜晚。

注：和 with 搭配的常用形容词：angry, bored, busy, careful, concerned, content, delighted, disappointed, familiar, frank, friendly, happy, honest, ill, indignant, patient, pleased, satisfied, strict 等。

(5) as concerns = *concerning* 关于。例如：

As concerns that matter, I don't think you are right.

关于那件事，我认为你是不对的。

Do you know the status of your products *as concerns* REACH?

你明白涉及到 REACH 的产品在你公司的地位吗？

(6) as for = *concerning, about, in the case of* 关于，至于；就…而言。例如：

As for you, I refuse to have any dealings with you.

至于你，我不想跟你打任何交道。

As for the economy, the road back to health will be long and painful.

至于经济，复苏的道路将是漫长而又痛苦的。

(7) as to 关于；至于；谈到。例如：

He inquired *as to* what the problem was. 关于存在什么问题，他进行了了解。

The police were searching for any clues *as to* his whereabouts.

警察正在搜寻有关他下落的线索。

The band's lawyer will advise *as to* which is appropriate.

这个乐队的律师会对哪个是合适的给出建议。

注: as for 和 as to 的区别:

❶ as for = *with reference to* (*sometimes meaning contempt or indifference*) 至于 (有时表示轻视或不关心)。例如:

You can have a single bed, but *as for* the children, they'll have to sleep on the floor. 你可以有一张床，但至于孩子们，只好打地铺了。

As for Mr Smith, I never want to see him here again.

至于史密斯先生，我永远不想在这里见到他。

❷ as to 放在句首，是为了加强语气。

❸ as for 只用于句子或分句句首，不用于句子或分句中间，而 as to 位置比较灵活。

❹ as for 后不可接句子，as to 不受此限。

❺ 突然想到的事情或提到的问题，使用 as for 来引导较为适宜；动名词短语也以 as for 来引导较为通常。例如:

Much pasture land is under water; and *as for* the grain, most of it has been ruined. 牧地淹了水；至于粮食，大部分也已毁了。(粮食是临时想到的，最好用 as for 来引导)

I could stay for two or three days; but *as for staying* for a week, it would be impossible.

耽搁两三天，我可以办到；至于耽搁一星期，那不行。

❻ 一般来说，不要用复合介词来代替 about, on, of 等一类介词。例如:

What's your opinion *about* my plan?

你对我的计划有什么意见？(句中的 about 不要用 as to 来代替)

(8) in the matter of 至于，关于；在…方面。例如:

We have no objection *in the matter of* salary. 至于工资问题，我们毫无异议。

(9) in connection with 关于…，与…有关。例如:

Tell me all you know *in connection with* that matter.

把你知道的关于那件事的所有情况都告诉我。

The police have arrested two suspects *in connection with* the bank robbery.

警察已逮捕了两名与抢劫银行案有关的嫌疑犯。

(10) in/with reference to 关于。**例如**：

He spoke *in reference to* the cowboys. 他谈了有关牛仔的事。

We would like to send you a sample *with reference to* the last shipment.
我们想要寄去有关上次交货的样品。

(11) as regards 关于。**例如**：

As regards the second point, we can discuss it at another meeting.
至于第二点，我们可以在下一次会上讨论。

(12) in/with regard to 关于。**例如**：

I have nothing to say *in regard to* that subject.
对那个问题，我没有什么要说的。

With regard to our quotation, we will discuss it later.
关于我们的报价，以后再讨论。

(13) in respect of/to 关于；就…来说。**例如**：

Workers will be paid *in respect of* their experience.
工人们将按照他们的经验获得报酬。

The teacher told stories about Washington and Lincoln *in respect to* the importance of being honest.
老师用华盛顿及林肯的故事做例子来说明诚实的重要性。

(14) in terms of 根据；就……而言。**例如**：

It is difficult to express it *in terms of* science.
要用科学的字眼来表达它是很困难的。

In terms of his professional abilities, he is just no match for you.
论工作能力，他根本不是你的对手。

注：关于 concerning, regarding, respecting, touching 这四个由现在分词转变而来的介词的用法，请参见 5 简单介词的用法。

3.2.18 表示排除的介词

表示排除的介词有：besides, beyond, but, except, except for, apart from, aside from, excepting, in addition to, with the exception of, bour, barring, save, save for, outside, outside of, ofter, exclusive of, over and above, among others, amoug other (things), other than, as well as, short of, on top of 等。

(1) besides

    ① *in addition to*，意为"除…之外"。例如：

    Besides milk and cheese, we need vegetables.

    除了牛奶和干酪外，我们还需要蔬菜。

    ② *except for*; *other than*，意为"除了…；而非"，通常与否定词连用。

    例如：

    We have no other dictionaries *besides* these.

    除了这些词典外，我们没有别的词典了。

    注：关于 besides, but, but for, except, except for 的区别，请参见 5 英语

        简单介词的用法详解的 besides, except 条。

(2) beyond = *in addition to*，意为"除…之外"，用于否定句和疑问句。例如：

    Beyond the coral reef, the open sea was dark blue.

    珊瑚礁之外的大海是一片深蓝色。

    Beyond that, there is nothing more I can say.

    除此之外，我再也没有什么可说的了。

    Have you got any other dictionary *beyond* this?

    除了这本外，你还有什么别的字典吗？

    He's got nothing *beyond* his state pension.

    除了国家发的养老金外，他一无所有。

(3) but 与 except 同义，两者的区别在于 except 强调被排除的内容，而 but
强调整体的内容，常与 no one, none, nothing 等否定词，who 等疑问词及
all, every one 等词连用。例如：

    There is no one here *but* me. 除我以外，没人在这儿。

    Who *but* Gloria would do such a thing? 除了格洛里亚还有谁愿意干这种事？

(4) apart from

    ① 与 except 同义。例如：

    All the children like music *apart from* Bobby.

    除了博比外，所有的孩子都喜欢音乐。

    ② 与 except for 同义。例如：

    This is a good book *apart from* a few mistakes.

    除了几个错误之外，这是一本好书。

③ 与 in addition to 同义，意为 "除…之外，还…"。例如：

Apart from the occasional visit, what does Allen do for his kids?

除了偶尔的一次探视，爱伦还为他的孩子做些什么？

(5) aside from 与 apart from 同义，主要用于美式英语。例如：

Aside from motorcars, the factory turns out bicycles.

除了汽车之外，这家工厂还生产自行车。

Aside from being fun and good exercise, swimming is a very useful skill.

除了有趣与良好的运动外，游泳还是个很有用的技能。

His writing is excellent, *aside from* a few misspellings.

除了几处拼写错误外，他写得很好。

(6) except = *with the exclusion of*; *other than*; *but* 除…之外。例如：

No food is left in the pantry *except* some bread.

食品柜里除了一些面包，其他什么也不剩。

I think no one can help me *except* you. 我想除了你之外没有人能帮助我。

(7) except for = *except*, *but for* 除…之外；要不是由于。例如：

The region is uninhabited *except for* a few scattered mountain villages.

除了几个零星的小山村之外，这个地区杳无人烟。

Tom is a nice person, *except for* his pettiness.

汤姆是个好人，就是有点小里小气的。

Except for him, I would be out of work. 要不是他，我早就失业了。

(8) excepting = *with the exception of*, *except* (用于句首或 not, without, always 后面) 除…之外。例如：

Excepting Sundays the stores are open daily.

除了星期天以外，那些商店天天都营业。

Everybody must observe the law not *excepting* the king.

人人都必须守法，国王也不例外。

(9) in addition to = *besides*, 意为 "除…之外，还…"。例如：

In addition to an album, I gave him a pen and a pencil.

除了一本照相簿外，我还给了他一支钢笔和铅笔。

In addition to going to the post office, I also went to the greengrocer.

我去了邮局，另外还去了蔬菜水果商店。

（10）with the exception of = *except*，意为 "除…之外"。例如：

I enjoyed all his novels *with the exception of* his last.

他的小说我都爱看，只是最后一部除外。

With the exception of the children, everyone was told the news.

除了孩子们外，每个人都被告知了那个消息。

（11）bar 除…之外；不包括…在内。例如：

This was your best performance, *bar* none. 毫无例外，这是你最好的演出。

She is the best singer in the world, *bar* none.

她是全世界最佳歌手，无人能及。

（12）barring = *apart from, excepting* 不包括…；除…之外。例如：

Barring accidents, I'll be there. 除非有意外，否则我一定会到场的。

Barring strong headwinds, the plane will arrive on schedule.

如果不是猛烈的顶头风，飞机会准点到达的。

The whole group was at the party, *barring* him.

除他以外，全组人都参加了晚会。

（13）save = *with the exception of, except* 除…之外。例如：

He answered all the questions *save* one.

除了一个问题之外，他回答了所有的问题。

All is lost *save* honor. 除荣誉外一切都丧失了。

I agree with you, *save* that you have got one fact wrong.

我同意你的意见，只是你把一个事实弄错了。

（14）save for = *except for* 除了…之外。例如：

The screen was all dark *save for* one bright spot.

除一个光点，屏幕上一片黑暗。

All drinks are included in the price, *save for* champagne.

除了香槟以外，所有酒水价格已经包含在内。

（15）outside, outside of: *with the exception of, except* 除…之外。例如：

Everything *outside of* the mind is objective reality.

除了思想以外，一切都是客观事实。

We have no other information *outside* the figures already given.

除了已提供的这些数字外，我们没有其他信息。

(16) after 除了…之外。例如：

After swimming, I like table-tennis best. 除了游泳，我最爱打乒乓球。

Nothing in our life, *after* health and virtue, is more estimable than knowledge. 除了健康与美德，人生再没有比知识更可贵的了。

(17) exclusive of = *not including* 不包括。例如：

The ship has a crew of 57 *exclusive of* officers.

这船上除高级船员外，还有57名普通船员。

All prices shown are *exclusive of* value added tax.

所有标价均不包括增值税。

(18) over and above = *in addition to* 除了…之外。例如：

The waiters get good tips *over and above* their wages.

除工资外，服务员还有不少小费。

He gets a number of perquisites, *over and above* his salary.

除了薪水外，他还有一些额外收入。

(19) among others, among other (things) 除…之外。例如：

This applies to, *among others*, promises to pay the debts of another and contracts concerning real property.

除了其他外，它适用于承诺支付他人的债务以及有关不动产合同。

He, *among other* things, talked about the present situation.

除了别的话，他还谈了当前的形势。

(20) other than 除了…，除…之外。例如：

There's nobody here *other than* me. 除了我这里没别人。

The old man wanted to see nobody *other than* his grandson.

除了他的孙子之外，这个老人谁也不想见。

(21) as well as = *in addition to*，意为"除…之外，还…"。例如：

She takes private pupils *as well as* teaching in school.

除在学校任教外，她也私自教授学生。

He knows my bad points *as well as my* good points.

我的优缺点他都知道。

(22) short of 除…之外；缺少。例如：

The recipe needed most vegetables, *short of* an onion.

除洋葱之外，食谱还需要大量蔬菜。

So, *short of* divorce, which I don't want, how do I deal with my feelings?

那么，除了离婚之外 (我不想离婚)，我该如何处理自己的感情问题呢？

(23) on top of = *in addition to, besides* 除⋯之外还。例如:

On top of borrowing 50 pounds, he asked me to lend him my car.

他向我借了 50 英镑，此外还向我借了车。

On top of this, several other benefits are being offered.

除此以外，还提供了其他几项津贴。

3.2.19　表示根据、按照、依靠、来源的介词

(1) at = *in accord with*; *following* 根据；遵循。例如:

I bought it *at* the request of my father. 我应父亲的要求买了这个。

At the invitation of a friend, he first came to Shenzhen for the 2004 Spring Festival. 应朋友之邀，2004 年他第一次来深圳过春节。

(2) by = *according to* "按照，根据"，与有些名词搭配具有隐含意义，不能仅从名词本身推断其含义。例如:

I am French *by* birth and a British subject *by* marriage.

我按出生是法国人，因结婚而成为英国国民。

They are cousins *by* blood. 他们在血统上是表兄弟。

She always does everything *by* the book. 她总是照章行事。

Sugar is sold *by* the pound. 糖是论磅出售的。

They are paid *by* the piece. 他们是按件计酬的。

The workers get paid *by* the hour. 工人们按钟点付给工资。

By my watch it is 2 o'clock. 按我的表，现在是两点钟。

He can predict a typhoon *by* rule of thumb. 他能凭经验预测出台风。

Some recognize others *by* the way they walk or *by their voice*.

一些人靠别人走路的姿势或说话的声音来识别。

Application letters from all over the country were pouring in *by* the thousands every week. 每星期数以千计的申请信从全国各地纷至沓来。

As a man is known *by* the company he keeps, so a tree *by its fruit*.

从所交的朋友就知道他的为人，从所结的果子就知道树的好坏。

(3) from

① *used to indicate a starting point* 用来表示 "起点、出处、出自、来自"。

例如:

All the characters in the book are drawn *from* real life.

书中所有的人物都来自真实的生活。

She borrowed a novel *from* the library. 她从图书馆借了一本小说。

We'll give you different topics to choose *from*.

我们将给你可以选择的不同题目。

② *used to indicate the source, basis* 用来表示"来源、基础"。例如:

He comes *from* Shanghai. 他来自上海。

He descended *from* a good family. 他出自名门。

We get light and heat *from* the sun. 我们从太阳取得光和热。

Never judge *from* appearances. [谚] 人不可貌相。

We must start *from* the beginning. 我们必须从头开始。

Success results *from* hard work. 成功来自努力的工作。

He received a letter *from* his friend. 他收到了朋友的来信。

What do you conclude *from* the facts? 从这些事实中你得出了什么结论?

From what was said above, I think this answer is right.

根据以上所述,我想这个答案是对的。

We hear *from* her now and then. 我们时常接到她的信。

She was extremely attractive, to judge *from* the magazine photographs.

从她在杂志上的照片判断,她长得极其迷人。

③ *used to indicate the cause, agent* 用来表示"原因、动因"。例如:

He acted *from* a sense of duty. 他的行动出于责任。

She suffered *from* cold. 她因受凉生病。

(4) in = *with the arrangement or order of* 按照某种安排或秩序。例如:

In his view, the bubble began around 2002.

按照他的观点,泡沫开始于 2002 年前后。

They all list the same days of the year *in* exactly the same order.

他们都按照同样的顺序准确的罗列了一年中的相同的日子。

(5) of

① *derived or coming from; originating at or from* 从…产生或来自…;源于或来自。例如:

men *of* the north 从北方来的人们

② *indicating origin, authorship* 表示 "来源、作者"。例如:

a man *of* humble origin 出身低微的人

the works *of* Shakespeare 莎士比亚的著作

He is a man *of* Chinese descent. 他是有中国血统的男子。

He was born *of* good ancestry. 他出生于名门。

③ *belonging or connected to* 属于…，与…有关系。例如:

the rungs *of* a ladder 梯子的横档

He is *of* a clinging sort. 他是那种要依靠别人的人。

(6) on/upon

① 表示 "依靠，凭借，由…支撑着"。例如:

They will go to school *on* foot tomorrow. 明天他们打算步行去上学。

The old man walked leaning *on* a stick. 这位老人拄着拐杖走路。

I had to live *on* bread and water when I was a student.

上大学时我只能靠粗茶淡饭生活。

I heard the good news *on* the radio. 我在收音机广播中听到这个好消息。

She told the children to pipe down while she was talking *on* the telephone.

她告诉孩子别吵了，她正在打电话。

② 表示 "根据，来源，基础"。常与 base, border, build, count, depend, found, lean, reckon, rely, rest 这类动词搭配。例如:

This story is founded *on* fact. 这故事是有事实依据的。

We rest *on* your support. 我们全靠你的支持。

You had better not count *on* clear weather this afternoon.

你还是不要指望今天下午会有晴朗的天气。

Children depend *on* their parents for food and clothing.

小孩依赖他们的父母供给衣食。

Such an act borders *on* folly. 这种行为近乎愚蠢。

We reckon *on* your support. 我们指望你的支持。

Judgement should be based *on* facts, not *on* hearsay.

判断应该以事实为依据，而不应该依靠道听途说。

We judge a worker *on* the basis of his performance.

我们以工作成绩作为评估一个工人的根据。

（7）under = *in accordance with*; *following* 根据，依据。例如：

The scope of investigations *under* the law is widening.

根据这项法律进行的调查正在扩大。

We shall issue a disaster bulletin *under* the order of the municipal headquarters of three controls.

我们将根据市三防指挥部的命令发布灾情公报。

（8）according to 按照；根据…所说。例如：

The trial proceeded *according to* the Chinese law.

审判是遵照中国法律进行的。

According to the facts in my possession he cannot possibly be guilty.

根据我所掌握的事实，他是不可能有罪的。

注：❶ 复合介词 according to 主要用来表示"根据"某学说、某书刊、某文件、某人所说等或表示"按照"某法律、某规定、某惯例、某情况等。例如：

He ordered his life *according to* strict rules.

他把生活安排得十分刻板。

According to my watch it is five o'clock. 照我的表，现在是五点钟。

Each man will be paid *according to* his ability.

每个人将根据他的能力获得报酬。

❷ according to 表示"根据"，通常是指根据别人或别处，而不能根据自己，所以其后不能接表示第一人称的代词（如 me, us），同时也很少接表示第二人称的代词（you），但用于第三人称（如 him, her, Tom, Mary, the doctor 等）则属正常用法。例如：

According to me, the film is wonderful.（误）

In my opinion, the film is wonderful. 依我看，这部电影很精彩。（正）

❸ according to 后也不接 view（看法）和 opinion（意见）这类词表示看法的词。例如：

According to my opinion, he did it very well.（误）

In my opinion, he did it very well. 在我看来，他干得很不错。（正）

（9）by dint of 凭…的力量，靠，凭借。例如：

He succeeded *by dint of* hard work. 他通过辛勤努力才获得成功。

The problems must be tackled *by dint of* education.

这问题必须靠教育来解决。

(10) by/in virtue of 依靠；由于。例如：

He became a champion at last *in virtue of* his perseverance.

凭着坚忍不拔的精神，他终于成为冠军。

The player defeated his rivals *by virtue of* greater experience.

凭借更丰富的经验这位选手战胜了对手。

(11) in accordance with 按照，依据。例如：

Do you always act *in accordance with* your convictions?

你是否一贯地本着你的信念行事？

Nature is rational, simple and orderly, and it acts *in accordance with* immutable laws. 自然界是合理的、简单的而且有秩序的，它是按照万古不易的规律行动的。

(12) in compliance with 遵照，依从，屈从。例如：

She gave up the idea *in compliance with* his desire.

她顺从他的愿望而放弃她的主意。

The company's financial statements are *in compliance with* generally accepted accounting practices.

公司的财务报表依从普遍接受的会计惯例。

(13) in consideration of 鉴于，考虑到；由于。例如：

They didn't give him heavy work *in consideration of* his youth.

考虑到他年轻，他们没给他分配繁重的工作。

I decided to do everyday exercises *in consideration of* my health.

出于健康的原因，我决定每天做一些锻炼。

(14) in deference to 遵从，听从；考虑到，鉴于。例如：

In deference to the wishes of her mother, Janet did not attend the dance.

珍妮特顺从她母亲的意愿，未赴舞会。

They were married in hometown, *in deference to* their parents' wishes.

他们遵从父母的意愿，在家乡结婚。

(15) in terms of 根据，按照；用…的话；在…方面。例如：

The cost was calculated *in terms of* the current price.

成本是以现在的价格计算的。

In term of money, he's quite rich, but not *in term of* happiness.

就钱来说他很富有，但就幸福来说就不然了。

(16) in the light of 按照，根据。例如:

He reviewed his policy *in the light of* recent developments.

根据最近的事态发展他重新考虑自己的方针。

The company has decided to review freelance payment *in the light of* the rising cost of living.

根据生活费用的提高，公司已决定调整自由职业者的酬金。

(17) in view of 鉴于；考虑到。例如:

In view of our long-standing relations, we decide to reduce the price.

鉴于我们长期的业务关系，我们决定降价。

In view of the increased demand for our products, we wish to appoint an agent. 鉴于对我方产品的需求有所增加，我方想委派一家代理商。

(18) on the basis of 基于，根据。例如:

Our policy should rest *on the basis of* self-reliance.

我们的政策要放在自力更生的基础上。

On the basis of our sales forecasts, we may begin to make a profit next year.

基于我们销售情况的预测，我们明年将开始赚钱。

(19) on the strength of 依赖…，凭借…。例如:

He got the position *on the strength of* his skill in finance.

他凭着自己的理财本领得到了这个职位。

He thought he might be offered the post *on the strength of* his father's former association with the firm.

他认为靠他父亲跟该公司的老关系，可能会得到这个职位。

3.2.20 表示否定的介词

表示否定意义的介词很多，有些名词或代词本身并不表示否定意义，但当它们与介词搭配构成介词短语时，就具有了否定意义。

(1) above 例如:

Her loyalty is *above* suspicion to us. 在我们看来，她的忠诚是无可怀疑的。

He is *above* taking profits for himself. 他不屑为自己谋利。

He was *above* all nervousness. 他一点也不紧张。

(2) against 例如:

We all need some savings *against* a rainy day.

我们都需要储蓄一些钱以备不时之需。

Everything seemed to be *against* me, but I fought back to my old position of strength. 一切似乎都不利于我，不过我努力争取恢复了我往日的实力地位。

(3) at 例如:

I'm determined to attain my purpose *at* any cost.

我决定为达到目的不惜任何代价。

He felt completely *at* sea in his new school.

他在新学校感到不知所措。

(4) before 例如:

Einstein was *before* his time with his ideas. 爱因斯坦思想超越了时代。

She desired no one for husband *before* him. 她非他不嫁。

(5) behind 例如:

I am *behind* him in mathematics. 我数学不如他。

The law is *behind* the times on a number of important issues.

这项法律就一些重大问题的条文规定已跟不上时代了。

(6) below 例如:

My brother is *below* my sister in ability. 我弟弟的能力不如我妹妹。

His income is well *below* the average. 他的收入远没有达到平均水平。

(7) beneath 例如:

Such behavior is *beneath* contempt. 这种行为令人不齿。

I felt that it is *beneath* me to argue with him any further.

我感到不值得与他争论下去了。

(8) beside 例如:

What you have just said is *beside* the mark. 你刚才所说的话不切题。

His remarks about gardening were *beside* the point.

他对园艺的言论简直是文不对题。

(9) between 例如:

What we said today is just *between* ourselves. 我们今天说的别告诉别人。

(10) beyond 例如:

The truth of the report is *beyond* all doubt. 该报道的真实性是无可置疑的。

The scenery there was beautiful *beyond* expression.

那儿的风景美丽得无法形容。

I'm afraid this old radio is *beyond* repair. 恐怕这台旧收音机不能修了。

His honesty is *beyond* dispute. 他的诚实是无可争议的。

（11）but 例如：

That's anything *but* true. 那绝不是真的。

His visit to Paris was anything *but* a success. 他的巴黎之行根本不成功。

（12）but for 例如：

But for your advice, I should have failed. 要不是你的忠告，我会失败的。

But for the rain we would have had a nice holiday.

要不是因为下雨，我们的假日一定过得很惬意。

（13）by 例如：

Global food shortages have taken everyone *by* surprise.

全球性的粮食短缺让所有人都猝不及防。

The policeman took the burglar *by* surprise as he opened the window.

当窃贼开窗子的时候，警察冷不防地捉住了他。

（14）despite 例如：

And *despite* himself, my friend began to relax.

我朋友不由自主地开始放松了。

There, *despite* himself, he was inveigled into making public his engagement.

在那里，尽管他不太愿意，还是受骗公布了他的订婚。

（15）for all 例如：

For all I care, you can throw it away. 你就是把它丢了，我也不在乎。

（16）from 例如：

His explanation was far *from* satisfactory. 他的解释一点也不令人满意。

Far *from* falling, the price of commodity goes on rising.

商品的价格非但没有下降，还继续上升。

（17）in 例如：

I am utterly *in* the dark about the matter. 我对这件事情完全不知道。

The plan is still *in* the rough. 这计划还不成熟。

（18）in spite of 例如：

In spite of our advice, he married above himself.

不顾我们的劝告，他同比自己地位高的人结了婚。

He laughed *in spite of* himself. 他不禁笑出声来。

（19）instead of 例如：

Instead of going bowling, let's stay home and play chess.

咱们不要去打保龄球，还是留在家里下棋吧。

We'll have tea in the garden *instead of* in the house.

我们将改在花园喝茶，而不在屋里喝。

（20）irrespective of 例如：

The laws apply to everyone *irrespective* of race, color, or creed.

法律对人人都适用，不分种族、肤色或信仰。

He rushed toward to help, *irrespective of* the consequence.

他不顾后果，冲上前去帮助。

（21）off 例如：

Keep *off* the grass. 请勿践踏草地。

When *off* duty I can do my private work.

不上班的时候我可以做自己的事。

（22）out of 例如：

It's *out of* the question to rebuild the tower. 重建那座塔是不可能的。

This kind of dress is *out of* style. 这种款式的衣服不时髦了。

He is a little *out of* humor today. 他今天心中有点不高兴。

（23）past 例如：

His mother's disease is *past* cure. 他母亲的病无法医治。

This is *past* dispute the best book he has ever written.

这本书无疑是他写得最好的一本。

The patient's condition is *past* hope. 病人的情况没有希望了。

She used to be a beauty *past* compare. 她曾经美丽无比。

The pair of shoes is *past* repair. 这双鞋子无法修补了。

（24）regardless of 例如：

I'll take the job *regardless of* the pay.

不管报酬多少，我都要接受这份工作。

Regardless of danger, he climbed the tower. 他不顾危险地爬上了高塔。

They decorated the house *regardless of* cost. 他们不惜成本装修这栋房子。

（25）under 例如：

My shirt cost *under* two pounds. 我的衬衫价钱不到两英镑。

All the children are *under* twelve. 所有的孩子都不满 12 岁。

（26）wanting ＝ *without* 没有。例如：

Wanting common sense, a man can do nothing well.

一个人缺乏常识，什么事也干不好。

His behavior was *wanting* in courtesy. 他举止没有礼貌。

（27）within 例如：

He stood *within* three meters of me. 他站在离我不足三米远的地方。

His house is *within* a mile of the station. 他的家距离火车站不到一英里。

（28）without 例如：

The day passed *without* accident. 这一天平安无事过去了。

The news report was completely *without* foundation.

这一新闻报道是毫无根据的。

3.3 介词的省略

在现代英语中，不用介词或省略介词的现象很普遍，在美式英语和口语中尤其如此。

3.3.1 时间状语前介词的省略

（1）在含有 this, these, that, those, next, last, some, one, any, every, tomorrow, today, yesterday 等时间状语之前常不用介词，有时用了反而被认为是错误的。例如：

Our firm is likely to reap a big profit *this year*.

今年我们公司很可能获得巨额利润。

The boys have decided to go camping *next week*.

男孩子们已决定下个星期去露营。

I'll start for shanghai *tomorrow morning*. 我明天早上动身去上海。

It must have rained *last night* for the road is wet.

路面是湿的，昨晚肯定下过雨。

We watched a fantastic play *yesterday evening*.

昨天晚上我们看了一场非常精彩的演出。

An active volcano may erupt (*at*) *any time*. 活火山随时可能喷发。

I'd like to see the pyramids in Egypt *one day*.

我希望将来有一天能见到埃及的金字塔。

You're welcome *any time* to my new place in London.

随时欢迎您到我伦敦的新家玩。

We get an automatic increase in pay *every year*.

我们的薪金每年会自动增长。

I'm sure your watch will turn up *one of these days*.

我肯定你的手表有一天能找到。

(2) 作时间状语的复数名词前可省略介词。例如：

Because she's a nurse she often has to work (at) *nights*.

因为是护士，她必须经常晚上工作。

In summer we go swimming (on) *Sunday afternoons*.

夏天我们星期日下午去游泳。

(3) 在 last, wait, live, stay 等延续性动词之后，表示时间长度的介词 for 通常可以省略。例如：

The war *lasted* four years before the North won in the end.

这场战争持续了四年，最后北方取胜。

I can't give these orders, unless you can *wait* some time or change the note.

我不能定这些货，除非你能等一些时间，要么就把这张钞票兑开。

I shall *stay* another three days. 我将再待三天。

注：在否定句中或用于句首时，介词 for 不能省略。例如：

For fifteen years he lived here. 他曾在这里住过 15 年。

I haven't seen you *for* a long time. 我很久没见到你了。

(4) 以 all, what, half 开头的名词短语作时间状语时，前面的介词通常省略。例如：

He remained a bachelor *all* his life. 他终生未娶。

This bottle of ink can last you *half* a year. 这瓶墨水够你用半年。

What time are you coming back? 你打算什么时候回来？

(5) 在有 the 并有后置定语的短语作时间状语时，介词可省略。例如：

Your film will be processed *the day after tomorrow*.

你的胶卷后天就可以冲洗出来。

Yes, very well. I saw them *the night before last.*

是的他们都很好，前天晚上我还看见他们。

They met *the spring of* 1989. 他们于 1989 年春相见了。

注：若无后置定语时，则介词不能省略。例如：

> They met *in the spring.* 他们在春天相见了。

3.3.2 表示年龄、形状、大小、颜色、价格等的介词省略

of＋年龄、形状、大小、颜色、价格等名词作表语、宾补或定语时，介词 of 可省略。例如：

We are (of) the same age. 我们同年龄。

The two books were (of) the same size. 这两本书一样大小。

(Of) What price is a single room for one night?

一间单人房住一晚多少钱？

The two sisters are (of) the same height. 这两姐妹一样高。

My vest is (of) the same colour as yours. 我的背心颜色和你的一样。

When I was a boy (of) your age, I could do it alone.

当我和你年龄一样时，我能独自做这件事。

3.3.3 介词 for 的省略

(1) 表示一段距离前的介词有时可省略。例如：

> They walked (for) twenty miles. 他们走了 20 英里。
>
> We traveled (for) fifty kilometers a day. 我们每天旅行 50 公里。

(2) 在某些结构中，表示原因的介词 for 有时可以省略。例如：

> Pardon me (for) *interrupting you.* 请原谅我打断你的话。
>
> They envy him (for) *his good fortune.* 他们羡慕他的好运气。
>
> I'll never forgive you (for) *that lie.* 我将不会宽恕你的那个谎言。

3.3.4 介词 on 的省略

表示星期、日期等时间的介词 on 可省略，尤其在新闻报道中。例如：

We'll arrive (on) *Thursday.* 我们将于星期四到达。

See you (on) *July the first.* 7 月 1 日见吧。

3.3.5 介词 at 的省略

(1) what time 前的介词 at 通常可以省略。例如:

(At) *What time* did he leave here? 他是什么时候离开这儿的?

(2) 在 about/around +时间名词前的介词 at 通常可省略。例如:

She arrived (at) *about ten o'clock.* 她大约（在）10 点钟到的。

We'll come (at) *around eight o'clock.* 我们大约在 8 点到达。

(3) at home 这一短语中的介词 at 在美式英语中通常省略。例如:

Let's stay (at) *home* this evening. 今晚咱们就待在家里吧。

3.3.6 介词 of 的省略

all/both/half 用于带限定词（如 my, the, these 等）的名词前时，其中的介词 of 通常省略。例如:

Are *all* (of) *the students* here today? 今天所有的学生都到了吗?

Both (of) *her children* go to the same school. 她的两个孩子在同一个学校读书。

The sea was rough and *half* (of) *the passengers* were seasick.

海面波涛汹涌，半数旅客晕船。

注: all, both, half 在人称代词宾格前, of 不可省略。例如:

It disheartened *all of* us that she had been dismissed.

她被解雇了，这使我们大家都很沮丧。

Both of them were voted out. 他们两人都落选了。

I'll eat *half of* it. 我要吃一半。

3.3.7 介词 from 的省略

在 prevent/stop...from doing sth. (阻止…发生), save... (from) doing sth. (使某人免受…) 等结构中的介词, from 通常可以省略。例如:

The heavy rain *prevented us* (*from*) *arriving* on time.

大雨使我们不能按时来。

Hard as the doctors tried, nothing can *stop him* (*from*) *dying*.

医生都尽了全力，依然回天无术。

If you do it tonight, it will *save you* (*from*) *having to get up* early.

假如你今晚做了这件事，明天早上你就不必早起了。

注：在被动语态中 from 不可省略。此外，在表示类似含义的 prohibit...from
doing sth. 中的 from 习惯上不省略，而在与此同义的 keep...from doing
sth. 中，from 不可省略，否则会产生歧义。

比较：$\begin{cases} \text{He kept me from working. 他不让我工作。} \\ \text{He kept me working. 他要我不停地工作。} \end{cases}$

3.3.8　介词 in 的省略

(1) 在 in this way, in that way, in the same way, in another way 等表达中的介词
in 通常可以省略。例如：

Do it *this way*. 这样做。

Let me put it *another way*. 让我用另一种方式解释。

(2) 许多动名词前的介词 in 可以省略。例如：

Be careful (in) *crossing* the street. 过马路要小心。

Bill lost no time (in) *telling* me about his idea. 比尔赶紧和我讲他的想法。

注：但若介词 in 出现在句首，则通常不宜省略。例如：

In crossing the street he was run over. 他在穿过马路时被汽车撞倒。

(3) 在以下一些常用句型中，介词 in 通常省略：

be busy (in) doing sth. 忙于做某事

busy oneself (in) doing sth. 忙于做某事

be late (in) doing sth. 做某事做晚了或做迟了

be long (in) doing sth. 迟迟做某事

spend money/time (in) doing sth. 花钱 / 时间做某事

注：这一结构在被动句中，介词 in 不可省略。例如：

The whole afternoon was spent *in* cleaning the house.

整个下午都用来打扫房子了。

waste money/time (in) doing sth. 浪费金钱 / 时间做某事

have luck (in) doing sth. 做某事时有运气

have difficulty/trouble (in) doing sth. 做某事有困难

have bother (in) doing sth. 做某事费劲

have a problem (in) doing sth. 做某事有困难

have a struggle (in) doing sth. 费气力做某事

have a good time (in) doing sth. 做某事很开心

have a hard time (in) doing sth. 做某事很辛劳

find difficulty (in) doing sth. 做某事发现有困难

take turns (in/at) doing sth. 轮流做某事

It is (of) no use / good (in) doing sth. 做某事没有用。

There is no difficulty (in) doing sth. 做某事没有困难。

There is no hurry (in) doing sth. 不必急于做某事。

There is no sense (in) doing sth. 做某事没有用 / 道理。

There is no use (in) doing sth. 做某事没有用。

There is no point (in) doing sth. 做某事没有意义。

注：在同样的结构中，如果使用 keep, deter, hinder 等动词，其后的 from 不可省略。例如：

He had to put up a fence to keep his cattle *from* roaming onto his neighbour's farm.

他只得筑起一道篱笆，使牛不走到邻居的农场里去。

Failure did not deter us *from* trying it again.

失败并没有能阻挡我们再次进行试验。

The crowd hindered him *from* leaving. 人群使他无法脱身。

3.3.9 连接代词和副词前介词的省略

在 ask, decide, depend, look, tell, certain, clear, sure, idea 等动词、形容词或名词后面，who, which, what, where, whether, how 等引导的从句中，前面的介词通常可以省略。例如：

Have you any idea (of) *when* they will come? 你知道他们什么时候来吗？

I'm not certain (of) *what* I'm supposed to do. 我不肯定我应该做什么。

It depends (on) *whether* you can afford it. 这要看你是否买得起。

Tell me (about) *what* she said to you. 告诉我她给你讲了些什么。

注：❶ 若以上从句被简化为"疑问词不定式"，其前的介词也可省略。例如：

I'm not quite clear (about) *what* to do next. 我不确定下一步要做什么。

❷ 除以上提到的少数情形外，在其他情况下则通常不宜随便省略。例如：

We're worried *about* where he is. 我们担心他现在在哪里。

3.3.10　其他情况下的介词省略

(1) outside of 与 outside 同义，作"除…外"解，of 可以省略。例如：

We have no other information *outside* (of) the figures already given.

除了已提供的这些数字外，我们没有其他信息。

(2) near to 与 near 同义，表示"接近／靠近"之意时，near 有比较级和最高级形式，介词 to 可以省略。例如：

He edged his chair *nearer* (to) the fire. 他把椅子移得更靠近火炉。

Please come and sit *near* (to) me. 请过来靠近我坐。

Pick a few apples from the nearest tree, the one *nearest* (to) the house.

从最近的树上，即从离屋子最近的树上，摘几个苹果下来。

(3) 在 give, sell, send 等带双宾语的及物动词后，介词 to 有时可以省略。例如：

He *gave it* (to) me as a present. 他把它作为礼物送给我。

It was the last one they had and they *sold it* (to) me at a knockdown price.

这是他们手中的最后一个，他们以低价卖给了我。

A new catalog of the merchandise was *sent* (to) him without delay.

立即寄给他一份新的商品目录。

(4) 在 tomorrow, tomorrow afternoon/morning/evening, yesterday, yesterday morning/afternoon/evening, today, tonight, nowadays 等前面，不用介词。

(5) 年或月前面的介词 in 有时可以省去。例如：

The book was published (*in*) May 1978. 这本书于 1978 年 5 月出版。

The book was published (*in*) 1978. 这本书于 1978 年出版。

(6) 当 once, twice, three times 等名词词组在句中作状语时，其前一般不用介词 for。例如：

I have read the novel *four times*. 这部长篇小说我读过四遍了。

Take the medicine orally *three times a day*. 这种药每日口服三次。

注：但 for the first time, for the second time 等在句中作状语时，介词 for 不省略。

The children were so excited to be taken aboard the plane *for the first time*. 那些小孩第一次被带上飞机，简直兴奋极了。

(7) 以 all 开头的表示时间的名词短语前，通常省略介词 for。例如：

In New York, some stores stay open *all night long*.

在纽约，有些商店通宵营业。

We have been on good terms with our neighbors *all these years*.

这么多年来我们一直和邻居关系很好。

She nagged at him *all day long*. 她整天唠唠叨叨地找他茬。

He is a rolling stone and got nowhere *all his life*.

他见异思迁，毕生一事无成。

(8) 在一些如 run, travel, walk, advance, extend 等具有"位移"含义的动词之后，for 表示持续时间或位移的距离，通常要省略。例如：

Charles *ran* (for) a mile in four minutes. 查尔斯在 4 分钟之内跑了 1 英里。

They *advanced* (for) twenty miles. 他们前进了 20 英里。

The celebrations *extended* (for) over three days. 庆祝活动延续了 3 天多。

(9) end up 后接动名词时，by 可省略。例如：

You'll *end up doing* time in the jail. 你将在监狱中度过余生。

(10) 在 on board 和 on this side 后通常省略介词 of。例如：

We went on *board* (of) Athens yesterday morning.

我们昨天早晨登上雅典号。

He crossed the bridge to *this side* (of) the river. 他过桥来到河的这一边。

(11) 在某些具体量词短语结构中，美式英语有时省略介词 of。例如：

a pair (of) trousers 一条裤子

one pack (of) cigarettes 一包香烟

(12) 在表示方式方法的短语中，省略介词。例如：

The passenger train is traveling (at) 250 kilometers an hour.

这列客车正以每小时 250 公里的速度行驶。

The Smiths cook (in) the Chinese style. 史密斯夫妇的烹调具有中式风格。

My luggage will be sent (by) express. 我的行李将用快递方式寄送。

(13) 在表示估量、重量的短语中省略介词。例如：

The water level rose (for) two meters in 24 hours.

水位在 24 小时内上升了两米。

Her son weighs (at) 25 kilograms. 她儿子体重 25 公斤。

（14）在 this/that way, one's own way 之前，常可省略介词 in。例如：

Should I go this way, or that way? 我应从这边走，还是从那边走？

That's Jack all over, he's got to have things his own way.

杰克完完全全就是这种脾气，想怎么干就怎么干。

（15）相同介词引导多个介词短语时，第二个介词可省略。例如：

Einstein cared little for fame and (for) money.

爱因斯坦不爱名誉和金钱。

Will you go to Beijing, or (to) Tianjing or (to) Shanghai this summer?

今年夏天你去北京，还是去天津，还是去上海？

4　介词搭配

4.1　短语动词

　　英语中的短语动词浩如烟海，不仅丰富多彩，含义微妙，生动活泼，而且极富表达能力。短语动词是我们熟练掌握和运用地道英语的难题之一。我们必须下大气力，通过大量阅读去真正熟悉和掌握短语动词，这不仅对阅读理解、翻译与写作能力的提高，而且对口头交际能力的提高，都大有裨益。

　　英语短语动词分以下六种类型：

　　（1）不及物动词＋介词：其作用相当于一个及物动词，宾语总是在介词后面。例如：

Never have I *come across* such a difficult problem. 我从未遇到过这样的难题。

She will *answer for* his safety. 她要为他的安全负责。

　　（2）不及物动词＋副词＋介词：其作用相当于一个及物动词。凡是三个词的短语动词，该动词必为不及物动词，居中的副词称为小品词，第三个词必为介词，宾语总是位于介词之后。例如：

The school wanted to *do away with* this rule. 这所学校想废除这条规章。

There are some things that teachers will not *put up with*.

有些事情教师是不会容忍的。

　　（3）及物动词＋副词：相当于一个及物动词。判断该动词是否是及物动词取决于其宾语。若宾语是代词，其构成形式为：动词＋代词＋副词。例如：

Thousands of people were at the airport to *see them off*.

数以千计的人在机场为他们送行。（off 在句中为副词）

They were so far away that I couldn't *make out* their faces clearly.

他们离得那么远，我没法把他们的脸辨认清楚。（out 在句中为副词）

His handwriting is so bad that I can hardly *make it out*.

他写得太潦草了，我简直看不清楚。（不可说 make out it）

　　注：❶ 如果宾语较长，则通常放在副词之后。例如：

　　　　I *filled in an application form*. 我填写了一份申请表。

（不说 I filled an application form in.）

❷ 有些这类短语动词既可作及物动词又可作不及物动词。例如：

The barrel of gunpowder *blew up*. 火药桶爆炸了。（不及物）

The soldiers *blew up* the bridge. 士兵们把桥炸毁了。（及物）

（4）不及物动词＋副词：相当于一个不及物动词，其后不可接宾语。例如：

The tall building *went up* in flames. 这座大楼在熊熊烈火中烧毁了。

The family *has* certainly *come down* in the world. 这个家族确实衰落了。

（5）动词＋名词＋介词：其作用相当于一个及物动词。例如：

He asked his neighbour to *keep an eye on* his house. 他请邻居照看他的房子。

We must *make full use of* our time. 我们必须充分利用时间。

The new facts *shed some light on* the matter.

这些新事实使这个问题有些明朗化了。

（6）be ＋形容词（包括过去分词作形容词）＋介词：相当于及物动词，宾语位于介词后面，形容词是短语动词的真正词义。例如：

I know he *is slow at* understanding, but you have to *be patient with* him.

我知道他理解力差，但你得对他耐心些。

He *is* well *experienced in* the way of the world. 他阅世颇深。

本书收集了大量常用短语动词，请参见附录一。

4.2 名词、形容词、副词、分词与介词的搭配

4.2.1 名词与介词的搭配

有些名词与介词搭配，相对而言是比较固定的，有些搭配则受到不同动词的制约，有些搭配则因使用的介词不同而其含义有所不同。例如 experiment 后面就可以跟 in, on, with 等介词，而含义有所不同：

（1）He made an interesting *experiment in* sound. 他进行了一项有趣的声学试验。

（2）The research institute conducted *experiments on* jet engines.

该研究所进行了喷气发动机试验。

（3）The steam engine was not invented until James Watt had made many *experiments with* steam.

直到詹姆斯·瓦特进行了许多次蒸汽试验以后，蒸汽机才发明出来。

①句中用介词 in, 意指声学方面的试验，不能用 on 或 with 代替；②句中用 on, 意指对 jet engines 进行试验；③句中用 with, 意指用蒸汽做工作介质对蒸汽发动机进行试验。

4.2.2　形容词、副词、分词与介词的搭配

和名词一样，不同的形容词要与不同的介词搭配，某些从名词而来的形容词，其搭配与该名词与介词的搭配大致一样。应当指出的是，某个形容词与若干个介词搭配时，含义也有细微差别。甚至可以说，若干个不同形容词与同一个介词搭配，该介词的内涵则是相同或接近的。例如:

I was *glad at* the news. 听到那消息时我很高兴。

She was *dismayed at* the news. 听到那消息她很沮丧。

再如，disappointed 后面可以跟: about/at (关于，涉及), 多指事情; in 后接表示人的名词，表示其行为、成就、性格等令人失望; of 表示原因或动机，指某人因被骗未得到其所期望或盼望的东西，多接抽象名词; with (对待，处理), 表示人与人或事之间的关系。例如:

She was *disappointed about* the weather. 她对天气感到失望。

We were very *disappointed at* losing the game.

我们因为输了比赛而感到很失望。

The students were *disappointed in* their new teacher.

学生们对那位新来的老师感到失望。

I'm afraid you're very *disappointed with* me. 恐怕你对我感到很失望吧。

I'm *disappointed with* my new computer. 我对新买的计算机感到失望。

He was *disappointed of* his hopes. 他因希望落空而感到失望。

My parents will be *disappointed in/with* me if I fail to get the master degree.

如果我得不到硕士文凭，我的父母将对我感到失望。

有关名词、形容词、副词、连词、分词与介词的搭配，请参见附录二。

4.3　成语介词

4.3.1　介词＋名词／形容词＋介词构成的成语介词

成语介词是复杂介词，一类多数由介词＋名词＋介词构成，个别由介词＋形容词＋介词构成；有些则由介词＋定冠词或不定冠词＋名词＋介词构成，后跟

宾语，在句中作表语、定语或状语。这类成语介词有：by means of, in spite of, on top of, within reach of, with the exception of, as a result of, with a view to, in common with 等。例如：

Stars twinkle *as a result of* the turbulent state of the air through which their light passes. 星星眨眼是由于星光透过的空气的湍流状态的结果。

In spite of the snowstorm, the test was administered.
尽管来了暴风雪，试验还是进行了。

The stock market was *on the brink of* collapse. 股市已到了崩盘的边缘。

I have a lot *in common with* my sister. 我和我姐姐有很多相同之处。

4.3.2　名词、形容词、副词、连词、分词＋介词构成的成语介词

这一类成语介词由名词、形容词、副词、介词副词、连词、分词＋介词构成，后跟宾语，在句中作表语、定语或状语。其构成形式为：

（1）名词＋介词：

　　a far cry from（与…大不相同；与…相距很远），avoidance of（避免）等。例如：

　　The climate in Alaska is *a far cry from* that of Florida.
　　阿拉斯加与佛罗里达的气候相差甚远。

　　We are *a far cry from* paradise. 我们离天堂很远。

　　One basic advantage of organization planning is *avoidance of* organizational inflexibility. 组织规划的一个基本优点就是可避免组织缺乏弹性。

　　We usually see *eye to eye on* the things that really matter.
　　我们对于重要事情总是看法一致。

（2）形容词＋介词：

　　due to, prior to, previous to, parallel to, subsequent to 等。例如：

　　The railway line runs *parallel to* the highway. 铁路线和那条公路平行。

　　On the day *subsequent to* the earthquake he went to Sichuan.
　　地震发生后的第二天，他去了四川。

（3）副词＋介词：

　　as far as, as far back as, as early as, conformably to（和…一致），differently from（不同于…），together with 等。例如：

　　She came *conformably to* her promise. 她按照约定来了。

These new facts, *together with* the other evidence, prove the prisoner's innocence. 这些新的事实连同其他证据已证明在押者无罪。

(4) 介词副词（小品词）＋介词：

down to, along with, up to, out of, apart from, aside from 等。例如：

Apart from showing technical proficiency, airline pilots must score well on psychological tests. 航空公司飞行员除了要展现技术精通之外，还必须在心理测试中成绩优良。

We were almost *out of* gas just as we found a service station.

正当我们找到一个服务站时，我们的汽油几乎用光了。

(5) 连词＋介词：

but for, because of, as to, as of 等。例如：

That means a $250 raise *as of* the first of next month.

那意味着从下月一日起加薪 250 美元。

They decided not to hold the meeting *because of* the storm warning.

由于暴风雨警报，他们决定取消这次会议。

(6) 分词＋介词：

according to, depending on, owing to, pertaining to 等。例如：

You'd better deal with these affairs *according to* priority.

你最好根据轻重缓急来处理这些事务。

Depending on the type of virus, it can simply clog up memory or, even worse, erase data. 依据病毒种类的不同，它可能仅仅是塞满内存，或者更糟糕的是，删除数据。

The coalmine was closed *owing to* exhaustion.

这个煤矿因矿源枯竭而被关闭。

Accountants record information *pertaining to* the economic aspects of an organization's activities. 会计人员记录有关某一机构活动的经济状况的信息。

有关成语介词，请参见附录三。

4.4 由介词构成的成语介词

由介词构成的成语介词，其特点是：它们在句中多作表语或状语；这些成语介词和复合介词不同，它们不是介词，而是介词短语，因此其后不能跟宾语。

这类介词成语有: as a rule (通常; 照例), at hand (在手边; 在近旁; 迫在眉睫; 即将发生), for nothing (免费), in no time (很快, 立刻), in vain (徒然, 枉然), on the hour (准时地), on the dot (准时), on the scene (出现, 到场, 在场), past question (毫无疑问的), to one's name (属于自己所有), without fail (必定, 务必) 等等。例如:

He met with troubles *without end.* 他遇到了无穷尽的麻烦。

With reservations I will recommend this film. 我将有保留地推荐这部影片。

Chief criminals must be punished *without fail.* 首恶必办。

有关介词成语, 请参见附录四。

5　简单介词的用法

下面讨论 100 多个简单介词的主要用法，并作一些用法差异的辨析。个别复杂介词如 out of 也当作简单介词，《朗文当代英语词典》(*Longman Dictionary of Contemporary English*) 就把 out of 单独作一词条。

abaft

at, toward, or in the direction of, the stern, or back part of a ship; behind 在船尾，向船尾，在船的后面；在…的后面。 例如：

abaft the mast 在船桅之后

Ships with square sails sail fairly efficiently with the wind *abaft*.
带有方形帆的船随风疾驰而去。

The captain was located just *abaft* the bridge. 船长就在驾驶台后面。

No smoking *abaft* the funnel! 烟囱后不准抽烟！

aboard

on, in, or into a ship, train, airplane, etc. 在船、火车、飞机等上。 例如：

She went *aboard* the plane. 她上了飞机。

He came *aboard* the car. 他上了车。

The captain is *aboard* the ship. 船长已上船。

Is there a doctor *aboard* the plane? 飞机上有医生吗？

about

(1) *on all sides of; surrounding* 在…四周；环绕。 例如：

I found an English garden all *about* me.
我发现我周围是一座英式花园。

We planted trees *about* the house.
我们在房屋周围栽了树。

比较：
The children sat *around* their mother.
孩子们围绕着他们的母亲坐着。
The children crowded *about* their mother。
孩子们簇拥在他们母亲的周围。

注：around 含有周围的观念较强，如上句含有"在他们母亲四周"之意；about 含有接近的意味较强，如上句含有"他们母亲的背朝着一面墙"之意。

(2) *in the vicinity of* 在…附近。例如：

He lives somewhere *about* the park. 他住在公园附近某处。

I dropped my key somewhere *about* here.
我把钥匙掉在这附近某个地方了。

(3) *almost the same as*; *close to* 差不多一样；大约。例如：

It's *about* ten o'clock. 现在大约十点。

He is *about* 30 years old. 他大约 30 岁了。

He weighs *about* 200 pounds. 他体重大约 200 磅。

The sitting room measures *about* 5 meters. 这客厅约有 5 米长。

(4) *in reference to*; *relating to* 关于…；关系到。例如：

This is a book *about* snakes. 这是一本关于蛇的书。

比较：
I know nothing *about* the matter. 我不知道这件事的内情。
I know nothing *of* the matter. 对这件事我全不知道。

注：about 所表示的关系，比 of 所表示的要详细些。of 用在 know, say, speak, talk 等动词后，表示关于某人某事物的存在；将 about 置于上列动词后，则表示关于某人某事物的详情。

(5) *occupied with* 从事，忙于。例如：

I must go *about* my business. 我必须忙我自己的事。

(6) *in the possession or innate character of* 在…身上或性格中具有 (神气、风采、派头等)。例如：

There is something of the soldier *about* him. 他有军人气概。

He has strong bureaucratic airs *about* him. 他官气十足。

注：about 此义，用于表示从外观上看得出来的模样、气派。至于需要体会才能感觉到的素质、特点则用 in。

比较:
> Is there anything wrong *about* me?
>
> 我有什么事做得不对吗？（外表活动）
>
> Is there anything wrong *in* me?
>
> 我有什么想法不对吗？（内心活动）

(7) *by or on the body of* 在身边，手头，例如:

Now almost everyone has a wrist watch *about* him. 现在几乎人人戴手表。

比较:
> Have you any money *about/on/by* you? 你身上带钱了吗？
>
> It's going to rain. Take this umbrella *with* you.
>
> 就要下雨了，把这把雨伞带着吧。

about, by, on, with 都有"在身边，在手头"的意思，一般可以互用，但其后的宾语若为较大物件时，如 dictionary 或 umbrella, 则只能用 with。

(8) *here and there in* 到处，在各处，和动态动词和静态动词均可搭配。例如:

He spent the whole afternoon walking *about* the town.

他用了整个下午在城里各处溜达。

He always leaves his books lying *about* the room.

他总是在房间里到处乱放书本。

(9) *on the point or verge of* 即将，正要。例如:

It is *about* to snow. 天就要下雪了。

The airliner is *about* to take off. 飞机就要起飞了。

注: be going to do 表示最近或很近的将来（immediate or near futurity）;
  about 只表示最近的将来，其后不能用表示时间的副词。例如:

She is *about* to leave here for Shanghai next *week*. （误）

She is *about* to leave here for Shanghai. （正）她下周要去上海。

above

(1) *over or higher than* 在…之上，比…更高。例如:

His conduct is *above* suspicion. 他的品行是无可怀疑的。

注: 上句中的 above = *beyond*, 但 beyond 更文雅。

This problem is *above* my comprehension. 这个问题我理解不了。

(2) *superior to in rank, position, or number; greater in quantity, degree, price than* 在级别、位置或数量上占优势；在数量、程度、价格等上比…更大。例如:

Tom is *above* average in his lessons. 汤姆的成绩高于平均水平。

He is *above* me in the class. 在班上他比我强。

She married *above* her station. 她嫁给比她地位高的人。

比较:
{
In rank he is *above* me. 在军衔上他高于我。
In rank he is *over* me. 他军衔高于我。
}

注: above 和 over 都表示等级在上，但有直接和非直接的区别。over 表示直接的关系，即隶属关系; above 则表示非直接的关系，即非隶属关系。

❶ 表示超过某数量的事物或人时，一般用 over 或 more than, 而不用 above。例如:

比较:
{
She has *above* thirty pairs of shoes. (误)
She has *over* thirty pairs of shoes. (正)
She has *more than* thirty pairs of shoes. (正) 她有 30 多双鞋子。
}

❷ 表示某数量或量度超过某水平时，可用 above。例如:

In this city the temperature in full summer is *above* 42 degrees centigrade. 这个城市盛夏温度高过 42 摄氏度。

These plants must be stored in the light at *above* freezing temperature. 这些植物必须储藏在冰点以上有光的地方。

❸ 放在句首多半用 more than 或 over, 而不用 above。例如:

More than 1100 square miles have already been burned and about 100 homes have been destroyed.

目前已有 1100 多平方英里的林地和约 100 处房屋被烧毁。

Over 1000 students jammed into the hall.

1000 多名学生挤进礼堂里。

(3) *in preference to* 偏好，优先。例如:

A miser loves gold *above* his life. 一个守财奴爱财胜过生命。

(4) *too honorable to bend to* 不屑于。例如:

I am *above* petty intrigue. 我不屑于要心机。

(5) *out of the reach of* 在…（法律）之上。例如:

No one in our country is allowed to stand *above* the law.

在我们国家，任何人不允许超于法律之上。

(6) up stream from 在…的上游。例如：

There is a small village *above* the stone bridge. 石桥的上游有个小村庄。

absent

without 没有，缺乏。例如：

Absent a legislative fix, this is an invitation for years of litigation.

没有一个明确的法令，这是引起这些年讼争的原因。

The gross value represents returns *absent* both taxation and interest on the investment's cash component.

总资产表示利润，没有征税和付给投资者现金部分的利息。

across

(1) *on, at, or from the other side of* 在对面，在另一边；从…的另一边。例如：

Her house is *across* the street. 她家在大街的对面。

She lives *across* the street. 她住在街对面。

注：表示"在…对面"，across from 与 from across 都可以说，美式英语多半用 across from，但两者含义稍有区别。

❶ across from 表静态意义，意为"在…对面"，与 opposite 同义，可省略 from。例如：

Just *across* (*from*) our house there is a clinic.

就在我们房子的对面有一家诊所。

The bookstore is *across* (*from*) the school. 书店在学校的对面。

❷ from across 则表动态意义，意为"从…的对面"。例如：

He beckoned to me *from across* the street.

他在马路对面向我招手致意。

They waved at us *from across* the room.

他们从房间那一头向我们招手。

(2) *so as to cross*; *through* 穿过；相交。例如：

The two lines pass *across* each other at right angles. 这两条线成直角相交。

注：across 和 through 的区别。

❶ across 和 through 均可用于从一定范围的一边到另一边的动作。across 的含义与 on 有关，表示动作是在某一物体的表面进行；

through 的含义与 in 有关，表示从某个空间"穿过"，涉及"体"的概念。

比较：
> He walked *across* the road carefully. 他小心地走过马路。
>
> I walked *across* the square to the café.
>
> 我步行穿过广场来到咖啡馆。
>
> I pushed *through* the crowds to the bar.
>
> 我穿过人群，来到柜台前。
>
> It took us three hours to walk *through* the forest.
>
> 我们花了三个小时才穿过这片森林。

❷ 有时 across 表示"横过"也可在"体"内进行，但此时它仍与 through 有差别：前者表示从某个"体"的一端到另一端，而后者表示穿过两端。例如：

He walked *across* the hall. 他从大厅的一端走到另一端。

He walked *through* the hall. 他穿过大厅。

❸ through 不能用于从"细而长"的物体 (如河流) 之一侧到另一侧的动作，要用 across。例如：

She swam *across* the river. 她游过河去。

(3) *from one side of to the other* 横过，越过，从…的一边到另一边。例如：

There are more than ten huge modern bridges *across* the Yangtze River.
有十几座横跨长江的现代化大桥。

The plane flew *across* the Sahara Desert. 那架飞机飞越了撒哈拉沙漠。

(4) *into contact with* 碰上，接触，与 come, run, fall 等动词连用。例如：

I came *across* my old roommate at the theater the other day.
几天前我在剧场遇上了我的老室友。

An idea came *across* my mind. 我突然想起了一个主意。

比较：
> There is a modern bridge *across* the river.
>
> 一座现代化大桥横跨这条河流。
>
> There is a huge bridge *over* the river.
>
> 一座巨桥屹立在河上。

注：across 指桥与河横成十字形；over 指屹立在河上 (rising above the surface of)。

afore

［古英语］= *before*，在…之前。可作连词或副词。例如：

And I'll be in Scotland *afore* ye. 我要先于你回到苏格兰。

Their son-in-law has gone to sea *afore* the mast. 他们的女婿当水手去了。

after

（1）*behind in place or order* 在地方或顺序之后。例如：

Day *after* day passed by. 日复一日地过去了。

Please line up one *after* another. 请按顺序排队。

Please close the door *after* you. 请随手关门。

注：after 指时间、次序的"在后"，指位置"在后"应用 behind，但在表示含有次序在后的意思的位置时，也可用 after，如上句。

（2）*next to or lower than in order or importance* 在顺序或重要性上次于或低于，亚于。例如：

Milton is usually placed *after* Shakespeare among English poets.

在英国诗人中，密尔顿通常排在莎士比亚之后。

（3）*in quest or pursuit of* 探求，追求。例如：

to seek *after* fame 追逐名誉

to go *after* big money 追求钱财

The policeman ran *after* the thief. 警察在追捕窃贼。

注：在 long, hunt, seek, search, research, endeavor, strive, gasp, sigh, lust, aspire, crave, yearn, grope, hunger, thirst, mad, eager, greediness 等动词、形容词和名词后，for 和 after 通用，但 after 的语气较重。

（4）*concerning* 有关，关于。例如：

Your uncle asked *after* you. 你叔父询问了你的情况。

（5）*subsequent in time to; at a later time than* 时间上在…之后；比…晚一点。

例如：

She arrived *after* three days. 她三天后到达了。

Five minutes *after* the fire, the firemen arrived at the scene.

火灾后五分钟，消防队员到达了出事现场。

比较:
- He will leave *in* a few days. 几天后他将离开。
- He left *after* a few days. 几天后他离开了。
- He will leave *after* three o'clock. 他将在三点后离开。

注: in 以现在为起点，表示时间（future space of time），用于一般将来时，不可用 after; after 以过去为起点，表示过去时间（future space of time），用于动词过去时。但 after 表示"时间的一点"，可以用于一般将来时，如上面的第三句。

(6) *subsequent to and because of or regardless of* 随后；因为；不管。例如:

They are still friends *after* all their differences.

尽管有许多不同之处，他们依旧是朋友。

She succeeded in solving the problem *after* hard work.

由于努力工作，她成功解决了那个问题。

She is very optimistic *after* all the hardships she has suffered.

尽管她遭受过那些艰苦，她仍然很乐观。

注: after 作此义解，通常和 all 连用，类似的结构还有 with all, for all。

(7) *in the style of or in imitation of* 仿照…的风格；模仿…。例如:

This fable was written *after* the manner of *Aesop*.

这则寓言是仿照《伊索寓言》写成的。

The two buildings are modeled *after* the same pattern.

这两座建筑是按照同一模式建造的。

(8) *with the same or close to the same name as; in honor or commemoration of* 以…命名，与…名字有相同或相近的名字；为纪念…。例如:

The boy was named *after* his uncle. 那孩子以他叔叔的名字取名。

(9) *according to the nature or desires of; in conformity to* 根据…的本质或愿望；与…一致。例如:

He is a man *after* her heart. 他是个合她心意的人。

against

(1) *in a direction or course opposite to* 与某方向或过程相反。例如:

We sailed *against* the wind. 我们逆风行船。

Drug taking is *against* the law. 吸毒是违法的。

(2) *so as to come into forcible contact with* 对撞，猛烈接触。例如：

We saw the waves dashing *against* the shore. 我们看到了拍岸的波涛。

The rain was beating *against* the windows. 雨点拍打在了窗户上。

(3) *in contact with so as to rest or press on* 倚在；紧靠着。例如：

He was leaning *against* a post. 他倚在一根柱子上。

(4) *in hostile opposition or resistance to* 反抗；抵抗；处于敌对状况或与…相抗衡。例如：

She struggled *against* fate. 她同命运抗争着。

(5) *contrary to; opposed to* 与…相反。例如：

against my better judgment 与我的判断相反

(6) *in contrast or comparison with the setting or background of* 对照；对比；以…为布景或背景。例如：

The pine trees were black *against* the morning sky.

在早晨天空的映照下，那些松树呈黑色。

(7) *in preparation for; in anticipation of* 为…作准备；期待着。例如：

The squirrels store plenty of food *against* the winter.

这些松鼠为过冬贮备充足的食物。

(8) *as a defense or safeguard from* 预防；防御。例如：

We are all taking medicine *against* the flu. 我们都在服药预防流感。

注：在有些地方，against 和 for 意思相近。例如：

It is necessary to provide *against* accidents. 有必要为避免事故作准备。

We must provide *for* the future. 我们必须为将来做好准备。

(9) *to the account or debt of* 以…抵付；以…兑换。例如：

The exchange rate of U.S. dollar *against* pound sterling is about two to one.

美元对英镑的兑换率大约是二比一。

(10) *unfavorable or injurious to* 不利于；对…有害。例如：

Public opinion was *against* him. 舆论对他不利。

(11) 表示方向，常与 over 连用，意为"在…的对面"。例如：

He lived *over against* the temple. 他住在那座寺庙的正对面。

(12) 表示对比关系，有时可与 as 连用，意为"而；与…相比"。例如：

The park opens five hours a day this year *as against* three hours a day last year. 这座公园今年每天开放五小时，而去年每天开放三小时。

along

(1) *over the length of* 顺着，沿着。例如：

We walked *along* the path. 我们顺着小路走。

They drove *along* the small roads and came to the woods.

他们沿着小路开车来到了树林。

(2) *on a line or course parallel and close to*; *in/during the course of* 沿着一条平行线或道路；在…过程中。例如：

He rowed *along* the shore. 他沿着海岸划船。

Somewhere *along* the journey I lost my hat. 在旅游过程中我把帽子给丢了。

(3) *in accordance with* 根据。例如：

The committee split *along* party lines over the issue.

由于各自坚持自己政党的路线，委员会在这个问题上产生了分歧。

alongside

by the side of; *side by side with* 在…旁边；与…并排/并肩。例如：

The ship lying *alongside* the pier was a mine-sweeper.

停靠在栈桥旁的那艘船是一艘扫雷艇。

The car was running *alongside* the train. 那辆小汽车正在和火车并排行驶。

The police car pulled up *alongside* ours. 那辆警车在我们的车旁停了下来。

Alongside the road was a field planted with maize.

路的两边是一片种着玉米的田地。

注：alongside 有时后接 of, 与 alongside 同义。例如：

My married daughter is living *alongside of* us.

我那结了婚的女儿和我们住在一起。

amid(st)

(1) *surrounded by* 被…包围。例如：

The soldier lost his way and found himself *amid(st)* the enemies.

那个士兵迷了路，陷在敌人包围之中。

This work was done *amid(st)* many interruptions.

这项工作是在许多干扰中完成的。

(2) *in the middle of* 在…中间。例如：

Amid (*st*) warm applause the honoured guests mounted the rostrum.

在热烈的掌声中贵宾们登上了主席台。

The airliner landed *amidst* the drizzling rain.

这架客机在蒙蒙细雨中降落了。

He drank off the wine *amid* the cheers.

他在一片喝彩声中把酒一饮而尽。

He was brave *amid* all dangers. 他在各种危险中总是很勇敢。

We lost our companions *amid* the storm and the darkness.

在暴风雨和黑暗中，我们失去了伙伴。

注：❶ amid 和 amidst 的意思相同，在英国多用 amidst, 在美国多用 amid。这两个词用于指位置、地点，比较少见，而多用于表示状况、情形或处境。

❷ among 指"混合或掺杂在多数可分离事物的中间"; amid (st) 却指"处在可分离或不可分离的事物中心而被包围"。如: among the crowd, crowd 表示群体，注重集合体中的各个体——在人群中间容易分别出来; amid(st) the crowd, crowd 是集合名词，把集合体作一体看——在人群中不容易分别出来。又如：

We noticed him *among* the crowd. 我们在人群中注意到他。

We detected him *amid(st)* the crowd. 我们在人群中侦察出他。

❸ amid(st) 带有文言色彩，在日常语言文字里不是很常见。

among(st)

(1) *in the midst of; surrounded by* 在…当中，在…中间；被…所环绕。例如：

She lives in a village *among* the hills. 她住在群山环抱的村庄里。

He lives in a house *amongst* the trees. 他住在一栋树木环绕的房子里。

(2) *in the group, number, or class of* 在…的一类、一组、一群或一个阶层中。例如：

She is *among* the wealthy. 她是个有钱人。

The Yangtze River is *among* the longest rivers in the world.

长江是世界上最长的河流之一。

He was only one *amongst* many who needed help.

他只是众多需要帮助者之一。

Mozart's compositions are undoubtedly *amongst* the world's greatest.

莫扎特的作品毫无疑问地被列入世界上最伟大的作品。

London is *amongst* the greatest cities of the world.

伦敦是世界上最大的城市之一。

The consensus *amongst* the world's scientists is that the world is likely to warm up over the next few decades.

全世界科学家达成的共识是：在未来几十年内，世界很可能变暖。

He found it *amongst* a pile of old books. 他是在一堆旧书中找到它的。

(3) *in the company of*; *in association with* 与…在一起；与…联合。例如：

I was traveling *among* a group of tourists.

我当时正在和一群观光客一起旅游。

Amongst relief workers, the immediate sense of crisis has moderated somewhat. 在救济工作者中，紧急的危机感已经有所缓和。

(4) *by the joint action of* 通过…联合行动。例如：

Among us, we will finish the job. 我们共同来完成这项工作。

(5) *with portions to each of* 分配，在…之间均分。例如：

I will distribute these apples *among* you. 我将把这些苹果分给你们。

(6) *each with the other* 互相之间。例如：

Don't fight *among* yourselves. 你们不要自相残杀。

注：❶ among 指三者或三者以上的多数同类的事物中间；amongst 与 among 同义，为文学用语。

❷ among 所指在其中间的多数事物，是可分别或可分离的，其宾语为复数名词或集合名词。

❸ among 可以表示多数事物中的一个或一部分，意思相当于 one of 或 a part of。

❹ amongst 与 among 同义，是 among 的变体。一般说来 among 总能替代 amongst, 而 amongst 则不然。请参见以上例句。

anti

opposed to; *against* 对抗；反对。例如：

I'm not *anti* the proposal; I just have some questions.

我并不反对这项提议，我只是有一些问题。

That's why you're so *anti* other people smoking.

那就是你如此反对其他人抽烟的原因。

They're completely *anti* the new proposals. 他们完全反对这些新提议。

注：anti 可作名词，表示"反对者，反对派"之意。例如：

They refused to join forces with the *antis*. 他们拒绝与反对派合作。

We have many supporters and a few *antis*. 我们有许多支持者和一些反对者。

around

(1) *on all sides of* 在…四周。例如：

The children planted trees *around* the field. 孩子们在那块地周围植了树。

(2) *in such a position as to encircle or surround* 处于这样的位置来环绕或围绕。例如：

The ship sailed *around/round* the world.

这艘轮船曾环绕世界航行。

The geologist lectured on the earth's revolution *around/round/about* the sun.

这位地质学家作了关于地球绕太阳运转的报告。

注：❶ 关于 around 和 about 表示四周或周围含义的差异，请参见 about 条。

❷ around, round, about 这三个词，常可互相通用，但上面例句2，就有所区别。around the sun 比 about the sun 含"轨道成圈形的状态"和"以太阳为中心点"等观念较为明确；round the sun 却仅指回转的运动。

❸ 一般而言，around 多用以表示围在四周的静止的位置，round 多用以表示环绕中心的运动，而 about 却不特别用以表示位置或运动。此外，around 多用于美式英语。

(3) *here and there, within; throughout* 到处，在…内的各处；遍及。例如：

They walked *around* the town. 他们在城里四处走动。

(4) *in the immediate vicinity of; near* 紧挨着；邻近。例如：

She lives *around* this university. 她住在这所大学的附近。

(5) *on or to the farther side of* 在较远一侧的或朝较远一侧的。例如：

The old man lives in the house *around* the corner.

这位老人就住在拐角那边的那幢房子里。

(6) *so as to pass, bypass, or avoid* 通过，绕过或避开。例如：

He managed to get *around* the difficulty somehow. 他设法避开了困难。

(7) *approximately at* 大约在。例如：

I usually wake up *around* six. 我通常大约六点醒来。

(8) *in such a way as to have a basis or center in* 以某种方式使之（成为）…的基础或中心。例如：

Our economy used to focus *around* farming and light industry.

我国经济曾经以农业和轻工业为中心。

The story was built *around* a famous film actress.

这个故事是以一名著名的电影女明星为原型写的。

as

(1) *in the capacity of* 作为…，以…的身份。例如：

He works *as* a driver. 他以开汽车为业。

I do not think much of him *as* a musician.

我认为他不是一位了不起的音乐家。

He is well known *as* an authority on the Hebrew scriptures.

他以希伯来文经典权威而著名。

This watch was given me *as* a birthday present.

这块表是别人送给我的生日礼物。

(2) *in the role of, taking the part of* 以…角色，扮演…角色。例如：

The illustration shows Sir Henry Irving *as* Shylock in *The Merchant of Venice*. 插图显示亨利·欧文爵士在《威尼斯商人》中扮演夏洛克。

(3) *in the function of* 以…的职务、角色、功能。例如：

in my function *as* chief editor 在我担任总编辑职位时

(4) *in a manner similar to; the same as* 以相似的方式；如同。例如：

On this issue they thought *as* one. 在这个问题上，他们意见一致。

United *as* one, the people of that country waged a war against aggression.

那个国家的人民团结一致，进行了反侵略的正义战争。

(5) *to introduce an example, or, more frequently, a list of examples*, 引出例子，或者更常见的是例子列表，表示"如，诸如"之意。例如：

Some animals, *as* dogs and cats, eat meat. 有些动物，如狗、猫等是食肉的。

In some words in English the initial h is not sounded, *as* honour, honesty, hour, etc.

英语中某些词的首字母 h 不发音，如 honour, honesty, hour 等。

(6) *in the form of* 以…形式。例如：

The ship first appeared *as* a mere speck on the horizon.

那艘船最初出现时只是地平线上的一个点。

We all start life *as* babies. 我们都是以呱呱坠地的婴儿开始人生的。

(7) *for the purpose of* 为…目的。例如：

The dykes were built *as* a protection against the sea.

堤坝的建造是为了防御海浪。

He only said it *as* a joke. 他说这只是个笑话。

(8) *as if one were* 好比是…。例如：

Although their daughter is in her early twenties, they still treat her *as* a child.

虽然他们的女儿 20 多岁了，他们仍然把她当作小孩对待。

The thief disguised himself *as* a policeman. 那小偷把自己伪装成警察。

(9) *When one was*, 当某人曾经是…。例如：

As a child, she was rather delicate. 她小的时候相当娇弱。

She showed me a portrait of her mother *as* a young woman.

她给我看了她母亲年轻时的肖像。

(10) *for the reason that* 因…原因（"as being" 省略）。例如：

We chose this one *as* the most suitable for our purpose.

我们选择这个最适合我们的目的。

The criminal was ordered to be deported *as* an undesirable alien.

罪犯被命令作为不受欢迎的外侨驱逐出境。

(11) *conveying in a rather vague way the idea of* "*to be*"，以相当含糊方式表达 to be（"是"）的意思。例如：

I immediately recognized the newcomer *as* the person who had accosted me in the street. 我立即认出那个新来者是大街上向我搭讪的人。

aslant

obliquely over or across 倾斜地横过或跨过

例如：

The sunlight fell *aslant* the floor. 阳光斜落在地板上。

The wrecked train lay *aslant* the track. 失事的火车横在铁轨上。

注: aslant 可作形容词或副词。例如:

If the upper beam is not straight, the lower ones will go *aslant*.

上梁不正下梁歪。

He leant *aslant* against the wall. 他身子歪斜着依靠在墙上。

The evening sunlight shone *aslant* through the window. 夕照斜穿入窗。

astraddle

so as to straddle or bridge; *astride* 跨着以便跨过或横过; 横跨。例如:

She sat *astraddle* a horse. 她跨在马上。

He was sitting *astraddle* a fence. 他当时跨在栅栏上。

astride

(1) *on or over and with a leg on each side of* 跨着, 两腿各在一边分开骑着。例如:

She sat *astride* the horse. 她两腿交叉坐在马上。

On the battlefield, soldiers *astride* elephants have trampled and terrified enemies.

在战场上, 两腿交叉骑在大象上的士兵践踏敌人, 使敌人胆战心惊。

(2) *situated on both sides of*; *lying across or over*; *straddling* 位于···两侧; 跨过、横过或跃过; 横跨。例如:

The city lay *astride* the river. 这座城市曾横跨河的两岸。

The bridge stands majestic *astride* the Yangtze River.

这座大桥巍然横跨在长江之上。

Lake Saint Clair is a lake in central North America, *astride* the border between southeastern Michigan and southern Ontario.

圣克莱尔湖是位于北美中部跨越加拿大安大略省南部与密歇根州东南部之间边界的一个湖泊。

Istanbul, formerly Constantinople, is a city in northwestern Turkey, the only city in the world that sits *astride* two continents—Europe and Asia.

伊斯坦布尔, 前称君士坦丁堡, 土耳其西北部的一座城市, 是世界上横跨欧亚两大陆的唯一城市。

（3）*in a dominant position within* 在…内处于支配地位。例如：

Napoleon stands *astride* the early 19th century like a giant.

拿破仑像巨人一样，在十九世纪初叶居于统治地位。

注：astride 可作副词。例如：

> Ladies ride horses by sitting *astride* or side-saddle.
>
> 女子骑马可以跨骑也可以坐横鞍。
>
> He rode *astride.* 他骑在马背上。
>
> Most of the figures in the painting are people striking the same pose, their hands held above their heads and their feet *astride.*
>
> 画面上绝大多数人物都是一种姿势，他们双手上举，双脚叉开。

at

（1）*in or near the area occupied by*; *in or near the location of* 在某一被占据地区里或附近；在某一场所里或附近。例如：

A red bus is stopping *at* the bus stop. 一辆红色的公共汽车停在了汽车站。

We arrived *at* our destination on time. 我们按时到达了目的地。

注：at 一般用于地点、处所；也用于指村庄、城镇等较小的地方。指城市、省、国家等较大的地方则用 in。但地方的大小是相对的，有时把一个大城市看作地图上的一个点，就可以用 at。例如：

> We arrived *in* Beijing early in the morning. 我们清早到达北京。
>
> Their plane arrived *at* Beijing in China. 他们的飞机抵达了中国北京。

（2）*in or near the position of* 在或接近某一位置。例如：

I spent my summer vacation *at* the seaside last year.

去年我在海滨度过了暑假。

比较：
> I met a friend of mine *at* the library.
> 我在图书馆遇到了我的一个朋友。
> I looked for an encyclopedia *in* the library.
> 我在图书馆找了一本百科全书。

注：❶ in 指地方范围内的广度（large extent of space），at 指某地方，表示空间的某一点（point of space）。在上面两个句子中，at 和 in 就不宜调换。参见上注。

❷ at 表示 "空间" 概念时, 不如 in 明确; 但 at 表示 "距离" 时比 in 明确。

比较:
> Mrs Smith is *at* the house.
>
> 史密斯太太在家里。(她没有出门, 不一定待在家里)
>
> Mrs Smith is *in* the house.
>
> 史密斯太太在家里。(她没有出门, 待在家里)
>
> An explosion was heard *at* the distance of 30 kilometers.
>
> 人们在 30 公里内听到了爆炸声。(远近比较明确)
>
> We heard an explosion *in* the distance.
>
> 我们听到了远处传来的爆炸声。(远近不那么明确)

❸ 作 "近旁、靠近" 解时, at 和 by 同义, 但有区别, at 是有意识的, by 是无意识的。例如:

My eletric bike is just *at* the gate.

我的电动车就放在大门口。(为了方便, 有意这样做的)

There is a big tree *by* the gate.

大门旁边有棵大树。(不是有意识种在那里的)

Mary is sitting *at* the desk to write a term paper. 玛丽在伏案写学期论文。(有意识的动作, 面桌而坐, 动词不定式表示目的)

Mar is sitting *by* the desk, reading a book. 玛丽坐在桌旁看书。(无意识的举动, 不一定面桌而坐, 也无需加表示目的的状语)

(3) to or toward the direction or location of, especially for a specific purpose 向, 朝向某一方向或位置, 尤指朝一特定目的、目标、方向等。例如:

Questions came *at* us from all sides. 问题从四面八方向我们袭来。

She is shooting *at* the target. 她正在瞄准靶子射击。

比较:
> He threw a bone to the dog. 他把一块骨头扔给了狗。
>
> He threw a bone at the dog. 他扔一块骨头砸狗。

注: to 表示 "给予" 的意思, 动机是善意的; at 表示动作及企图攻击的目标, 动机是恶意的。又如:

He shot the man. 他射杀了那个人。

He shot *at* the man. 他朝那个人开枪射击。(可能未击中)

at 的这种涵义对于其他动词来说也是如此。

(4) *present during; attending* 出席。例如：

She was present *at* the dance. 她出席了舞会。

He is now *at* a meeting in the city. 他在城里参加了一个会议。

(5) *within the interval or span of* 在···期间，在某一时间间隔或时间跨度内。例如：

Keep such men *at* a distance. 不要与这种人接近。

He comes to see me *at* intervals. 他时常来看我。

(6) *in the state or condition of* 在某一状态或状况下。例如：

She was *at* peace with her conscience. 她感到心安理得。

I was *at* a loss what to do. 我茫然不知做什么。

(7) *in the activity or field of* 在某一活动或某一领域内。例如：

Citizens are entitled *at* law to criticize the government functionaries.

公民在法律上有权批评政府工作人员。

He is skilled *at* playing chess. 他精于棋艺。

(8) *to or using the rate, extent, or amount of; to the point of* 在某一点到达或运用比率、限度或数量；在某一点（常与形容词最高级连用）。例如：

The shuttle, Columbia, was flying *at* about 20,000 kilometers an hour.

哥伦比亚号航天飞机正以每小时约 20000 公里的速度飞行。

Our population is growing *at* a slower rate.

我们的人口以较慢的速度增长。

比较：

- I bought the two books *at* 20 dollars.
  我以 20 美元的价格买下了那两本书。
- I bought the two books *for* 20 dollars.
  我花了 20 美元买了那两本书。

注：❶ at 用来表示比率、价值、价格等义；指整个价钱时，用 for。例如：

She is *at* the zenith of her career. 她正处在事业的顶峰。

She is a singer *at* best. 她充其量是个歌手。

❷ at 常与形容词最高级或某些表示最高或最低含义的名词连用。例如：

at first, *at* last, *at* best, *at* worst, *at* most, *at* the lowest, *at* all, *at* the top (of), *at* the bottom (of), *at* the summit（在顶峰）等。

(9) *(of time) on, near, or by the time or age of*（指时间）达到、接近某一时刻或节日，年节。例如：

at three o'clock 三点钟

at dawn/dusk/noon/sunrise/sunset/night/dinner time/midnight

拂晓 / 黄昏 / 中午 / 日出 / 日落 / 晚上 / 晚饭时间 / 午夜

at 72 years of age 到七十二岁时

at Christmas/Easter 在圣诞节 / 复活节

注: ❶ 表示时间的一点用 at, 如 *at* seven o'clock, *at* noon; 表示一段时间用 on 或 in, 一般而言, 指某天用 on, 如 *on* Monday, *on* the first day of June; 指长于或短于一天的一段时间用 in, 如 *in* the morning, *in* a week, *in* a month, *in* the last century 等。

❷ 表示某天的朝夕用 on, 如 *on* Sunday morning, *on* the afternoon of October the first。如果在 morning, afternoon 之前有形容词也需用 on, 如 *on* a fine morning, *on* a quiet evening 等。

❸ 在表示不确定的时间和短期假日的名词之前用 at, 如 *at* that time, *at* lunch time, *at* night, *at* Christmas（但 on Christmas Day）, at the weekend（美式英语用 on the weekend）等。

❹ 如果某月某日在上（下）午前有 early, late 等修饰语, 介词仍用 in, 如 *in* the late afternoon of 1st December。

(10) *on account of*; *because of* 因为。例如:

The baby stopped crying *at* the sight of its mother. 婴儿看到母亲就不哭了。

We rejoiced *at* the victory. 我们因胜利而欢欣鼓舞。

比较:{She was frightened *at* the noise. 她一听到那声音就害怕。
She was frightened *of* him. 她害怕他。

注: at 意为 "听见或看见…大吃一惊", 用来表示偶然受外界的刺激而引起的高兴、恐惧等义; of 用来表示日常的或习惯上已具有的心理状态。

比较:{What are you angry *at/about*? 你在为什么事生气?
She was angry *with* me for saying so. 她因为我那样说而生气。

注: angry at/about 后接事物; angry with 后接人。对于其他的形容词也有这种区别。

(11) *by way of*; *through* 以…方式; 通过

Smoke comes out *at* the windows. 烟从窗户冒出来。

I entered *at* the front door. 我从前门走了进去。

We walked ten kilometers *at* a stretch. 我们一口气走了 10 公里。

(12) *in accord with; following; dependent on* 根据；遵循；凭借。例如：

I did it *at* her request. 我是应她的请求做的。

The juvenile delinquent was set free *at* the mercy of the court.

这个少年犯在法庭的宽容下被释放。

(13) *occupied with* 从事，忙于。例如：

The sea was *at* work. 大海波涛汹涌。

He died *at* his post. 他殉于职守。

athwart

(1) *from one side to the other of; across* 从一侧到另一侧；穿过。例如：

the Stars that shoot athwart the Night (Alexander Pope)

划破夜空的星星（亚历山大·波普）

They threw a bridge *athwart* the river. 他们在这条河上架了一座桥。

The ship was anchored *athwart* the harbour mouth. 那轮船横着停泊在港口。

The pagoda cast its shadow *athwart* the lake. 塔影斜映在湖面上。

The ship sailed *athwart* our path. 那条船横穿驶过我们的航道。

(2) *contrary to; against* 相反；相对。例如：

His tendency toward violence was *athwart* the philosophy of the peace movement. 他倾向于用暴力，这可是跟和平运动的宗旨背道而驰的。

Everything is going on *athwart* the wishes of our friends.

事事都阻碍我朋友们的愿望。

注：athwart 可作副词。例如：

Everything goes *athwart* with him. 他事事不如意。

atop

on the top of 在…顶上。例如：

atop the flagpole 在旗杆顶上

He had a hat *atop* his head. 他头上有顶帽子。

A seagull perched *atop* the mast. 一只海鸥停歇在桅杆顶上。

The picture shows us *atop* a high hill. 这张照片里我们站在高山顶上。

A tuft of grass *atop* the wall sways right and left in the wind.

墙上一棵草，风吹两边倒。

注: atop 可作副词。例如:

> He climbed *atop*. 他爬到了顶上。

bar

except for, excluding, but 除…之外；不包括…在内。例如:

This was your best performance, *bar* none. 毫无例外，这是你最好的演出。

He is the best student *bar* none. 他是最好的学生，无人可比。

We were all invited *bar* none. 我们无一例外地都受到了邀请。

注: 除了在一些传统的短语和结构外，bar 已不通用，如以上例句中的 bar
none = without any exception, 作 "无例外" 解。

barring

apart from the occurrence of; *excepting*; *if there is/are not* 不包括…；除…之外；
如果没有。例如:

Nobody else knows *barring* you and me. 除你我之外无人知道。

Barring strong headwinds, the plane will arrive on schedule.

如果不是猛烈的顶头风，飞机会准点到达的。

The whole group was at the party, *barring* him.

除他以外，全组人都参加了晚会。

We shall return at midnight, *barring* accidents.

除非有意外事故，我们将于午夜回来。

We should arrive in half an hour, *barring* holdups.

若无交通阻塞，我们半小时后可到达。

before

(1) *previous to in time; earlier than* 在…时间之前；早于…。例如:

> the night *before* last 前晚
>
> Darwin was *before* his time with his ideas.
>
> 达尔文思想超越了时代。

比较:
- The moon will not rise *for* an hour.
  月亮过一小时才升起来。
- The moon will (not) rise *before* one o'clock.
  月亮一点钟以前(不)会升起来。

注：❶ for 用在否定句中，表示一段时间；before 可以用于肯定句或否定句中，但只表示时间的一点，这与 after 用法相同。before an hour 或 before three minutes 都是不正确的用法。

❷ 有些语法书上说，在否定句中，before 和 till 或 until 可以互相换用，但应指出，句子含义不尽相同。

比较:
- I didn't go to bed *before* midnight.
  我不曾在半夜以前就寝。(在半夜或半夜过后才就寝)
- I didn't go to bed *till/until* midnight. 我直到半夜才就寝。

❸ 火灾发生前10分钟，她离开了这家旅馆。

这句话的正确译法是：

Ten minutes *before* the fire, she left the hotel.

(2) *in front of* 在⋯前面。例如:

The interests of the country stand *before* the interests of the individuals.

国家利益高于个人利益。

He sat just *before* me. 他就坐在我的前面。

比较:
- He is sitting *before/behind* us. 他坐在我们的前面 / 后面。
- There is an old pine tree *in front of* the hotel.
  旅馆的前面有一颗古松树。

注：表示在建筑物的前面或后面，不用 before 或 behind, 而用 in front of 或 at the back of (英式英语), at/in the rear of (美式英语)。

(3) *in store for; awaiting* 即将发生的；等待着。例如:

Pride goes *before* a fall. 骄傲必败。

A young person's whole life lies *before* him.

年轻人的整个一生展现在他前面。

(4) *into or in the presence of* 进入，在⋯面前。例如:

She asked that the visitor be brought *before* her.

她要求把访问者带到她的面前来。

(5) *under the consideration or jurisdiction of* 在考虑中，在审理中。例如：

The case is now *before* the court. 这个案子现在已交庭审理。

(6) *in a position superior to* 地位高于。例如：

The prince is *before* his brother in the line of succession.

在王位继承权上，这个王子优于他的兄弟。

(7) *in preference to*; *rather than* 与其…宁可。例如：

She desired no one for husband *before* him. 她非他不嫁。

He would die *before* betraying his country. 他宁死也不背叛自己的国家。

behind

(1) *at the back of or in the rear of* 在…之后，在…后面，在…的后部。例如：

He sat *behind* her. 他坐在她后面。

比较：
{
Shut the door *after* you.
Shut the door *behind* you.
}

注：第一句的意思是："随手关门"，after 含有运动的意味；第二句的意思是："关上你背后的门"，behind 表示静止的位置。

(2) *in a place or time that has been passed or left by* 处于已过去的或被留下的时间或地点。例如：

Their worries are *behind* them. 他们的烦恼已过去。

He has left a sweet memory *behind* him. 他留下了甜蜜的回忆。

(3) *later than* 迟于…。例如：

The plane was *behind* schedule. 飞机晚点了。

比较：
{
The train was *behind* time. 火车晚点了。
He is *behind* the times. 他落后于时代了。
}

注：behind time 意为"晚点"；behind the times "落在时代的后面"。

(4) *used to indicate deficiency in performance*; *in an inferior position to* 不足；落后。例如：

She is *behind* none of them in her studies.

她在学习上不落后于他们中的任何人。

(5) *hidden or concealed by* 被…隐藏、掩盖。例如：

There must be something *behind* it. 其中必有隐情。

(6) *in the background of*; *underlying* 在…背后；隐含的。例如：

Behind your every action is self-interest. 你的每一个行动都出于个人私利。

(7) *in a position of support*; *at the back of* 处于支持位置；做后盾。例如：

Don't be afraid. We're all *behind* you. 不用怕，我们大家都支持你。

(8) in pursuit of 追求，追赶。例如：

The police were hard *behind* the escapees. 警察正在紧追逃犯。

below

(1) *underneath*; *beneath* 在…下面；在…下方。例如：

The sun has gone *below* the horizon. 太阳已经落到地平线以下了。

比较：{ We saw the valley *below* us. 我们看到了下面的山谷。
       He took shelter from the rain *under* a tree. 他在树下躲雨。

注：under 表示处于垂直线的下面；below 仅表示位置低于所提及的事物。

(2) *lower than, as on a graduated scale* 在…以下，如刻度尺上标示的以下。例如：

The temperature today is *below* zero. 今天的温度在零度以下。

He was *below* her in intelligence. 他的智力比她低。

(3) *down stream from* 在…的下游。例如：

The river *below* the bridge is in flood. 桥下的河流泛滥了。

(4) *lower than or not sufficient in degree, amount, weight* (程度、数量、重量等) 不足、不满，在…以下。例如：

The number of students in this university is *below* ten thousand.
这所大学的学生人数不足一万。

Her salary is *below* the average. 她的工资低于平均数。

(5) *unsuitable to the rank or dignity of* 有失身份的；与尊严不合适的。例如：

Such petty behavior is *below* me. 如此卑劣的行为有失我的身份。

比较：{ My brother is in the class *below* me.
       My brother is in the class *beneath* me.

注：below 和 beneath 可通用，但 beneath 的语气强些。the class below me 仅表示说话者叙述"低我一班"这一事实而别无其他意思；the class beneath me 却显示了说这句话的人的自我优越感，并对对方含有轻蔑的意味。

beneath

(1) *lower than*; *below* 低于；在···下方。例如：

Shall we rest in the shade *beneath* these trees?

我们在树下荫凉处休息一下好吗?

(2) *covered or concealed by* 被···覆盖，被···隐藏。例如：

The earth lay *beneath* a blanket of snow. 大地被厚厚的白雪覆盖。

(3) *under the force, control, or influence of* 在···力量、控制或影响之下。例如：

We shall do well *beneath* his guiding hand.

在他的指导下，我们将做得很好。

(4) *lower than, as in rank or station* 低于···，如在等级或地位上低于。例如：

A captain is *beneath* a major. 上尉低于少校。

(5) *unworthy of*; *unbefitting* 不值得；有损于。例如：

It would be *beneath* him to do that. 他做那件事未免有失身份。

It was *beneath* me to beg. 不值得我去乞求。

注：beneath 一般多用于抽象意义，而 under 和 below 多用于具体意义，
见以上两句。beneath 表示具体"在下"意义时，常见于文学体裁，
这时 beneath 和 under, below 的用法相似。例如：

Beneath the moon everything was still. 月光下面万籁俱寂。

Let us rest ourselves here *under* these trees.

让我们在树下休息一会儿吧。

beside

(1) *at the side of*; *next to* 在···旁边；挨着。例如：

There is a reading-lamp *beside* his bed. 他床边有一盏台灯。

比较：
┌ They sat *at* the desk.
┤ They sat *beside/by* the desk.
└ They stood *by* me.

注：❶ at 表示有目的接近；beside 和 by 表示偶然的靠近，但 by 比
beside 语势较强，多用于日常的用语中。

❷ to stand by one 意为"帮助某人"，如果要说站在某人旁边，以 to
stand beside one 来表达为妥当。

(2) *in comparison with* 与…相比较。例如：

This is a proposal that seems quite reasonable *beside* the others.

这是一个与其他相比似乎相当合理的建议。

The refrigerators of this factory can be ranked *beside* the best of their kind in the world. 这家工厂的冰箱比得上国际上最好的同类产品。

(3) *on an equal footing with* 与…平等。例如：

He has earned a place *beside* the best performers in the business.

他在商业中赢得了与最佳者平等的地位。

(4) in addition to 除…之外。例如：

Many creatures *beside* man live in communities.

除人类之外，许多生物也是群居的。

注：现代用法中，"除…之外"和"除了…外"的意思更常用 besides，而较少用 beside 来表达。

(5) *not relevant to* 与…无关。例如：

He argued *beside* the point. 他的议论离题了。

(6) *in a state of extreme excitement or agitation* 发狂；处于异常兴奋或激动状态，与反身代词连用。例如：

They were *beside* themselves with delight. 他们欣喜若狂。

He was *beside* himself with anger. 他怒不可遏。

besides

(1) in addition to 除…之外 。例如：

Besides milk and cheese, we need vegetables.

除了牛奶和干酪外，我们还需要蔬菜。

(2) except for; other than 除了… ；而非，通常与否定词连用。例如：

We have no other dictionaries *besides* these.

除了这些辞典外，我们没有别的辞典了。

注：❶ besides 和 except 都含"除…外"的意思。besides 表示一种累加关系，指"除…外，另外还有"，着重"另外还有"。例如：

I have five other books *besides* this. 除这本以外，我还有五本别的书。

❷ except 或 but 表示一种排除关系，意指"除了什么之外，不再有…"，即"从整体里减去一部分"，着重于"排除在外"。例如：

We all went there *except* Mary. 除了玛丽外，我们都到那儿去了。

❸ 在否定句中，besides 也表示"除…之外，不再有… "，与 but, except 同义，可以通用。例如：

No one passed the exam *besides/except* Tom.

除汤姆外，没一个人通过考试。

There is nothing on the desk *except/besides* a textbook.

课桌上除了一本教科书之外，什么也没有。

❹ but 与 except 的区别：两者都可表示"除…外，不再有…"，但含义上略有差别。but 侧重指意义的几乎完整性，而 except 则侧重指后面除去的部分。

比较：
- All are here *but* one. 除一个人都到了。
- All are here *except* one. 还有一个人没到。

❺ 在现代英语中，but 的介词用法十分有限，一般说来，它只能用在下列词语之后：no, no one, nobody, nothing, nowhere 等；any, anyone, anybody, anything, anywhere 等；every, everyone, everybody, everything, everywhere 等；all, none 等；who, what, where 等。例如：

Everyone knows it *but* you. 除你之外大家都知道。

No one but he showed much interest in it.

除他之外，没有一个人对此表现出很大兴趣。

❻ 一般说来，如果没有出现上述词汇，就不宜使用介词 but，否则可能造成病句。但 except 却没有以上限制。

比较：
- The window is never opened *but* in summer. （误）
- The window is never opened *except* in summer. （正）
- 除夏天外，这扇窗户从不打开。

❼ except for 用于句首时，与 except 同义，但 except for 不表示部分与整体之间的关系，换句话说，包括的与不包括的内容在性质上是不同的；或者，只是对所述的情况进行修正或补充细节。例如：

I can do nothing *except for* swimming in the dog days.

在三伏天里，除了游泳，我什么事也不做。

The place where I live is very quiet *except for* occasional chirps and twitters of birds.

我住的地方很宁静，只是偶尔听到鸟儿叽叽喳喳的叫声。

between

(1) *in or through the position or interval separating* 在分离的位置或时间之间。例如:

They are building a railroad *between* the two cities.

他们正在修建一条连接两座城市之间的铁路。

She arrived *between* 6 and 7 last night. 她是在昨晚 6 点到 7 点到的。

(2) *intermediate to, as in quality, amount, or degree* 在质量、数量或程度上居于…中间。例如:

The chair costs *between* 15 and 20 dollars.

这把椅子的价值在 15 美元到 20 美元。

(3) *amidst* 交集于…之间，多用于连接抽象名词。例如:

Between astonishment and joy, she couldn't help bursting into tears.

她惊喜交加，控制不住自己放声大哭起来。

(4) *associating or uniting in a reciprocal action or relationship* 在互惠行为或关系中与…联系。例如:

The negotiations led to an agreement *between* the workers and the management.

谈判导致工人们与管理者之间达成了一项协议。

(5) *in regard to the respective natures or qualities of; as to distinguish between right and wrong* 识别，区别。例如:

I can make a clear distinction *between* the two.

我能清楚地辨别这两个的不同。

(6) *by the combined effort or effect of* 由于共同努力的结果。例如:

Between them they succeeded. 由于共同努力，他们成功了。

(7) *in the combined ownership of* 共同拥有。例如:

They had only a few dollars *between* them. 他们总共只有几美元。

She shared the oranges *between* the three children.

她把橘子分给这三个孩子。

(8) *as measured against, often used to express a reciprocal relationship* 权衡;与…做比较。通常用于表示一种互相的关系。例如:

We have to choose *between* riding and walking.

我们必须在搭车和走路之间选择。

注：❶ between 和 among 都含有 "在…中间" 的意思。among 用于 "三者或三者以上之间"。例如：

He often went *among* the masses. 他经常深入群众。

❷ between 虽然多用于 "两者之间"，但有时也可用于 "三者或三者以上之间"，指每个人或物与别的每个人或物各自之间的关系。例如：

a trade agreement *between* Great Britain, France and the United States 一项英国、法国和美国之间的贸易协定

❸ 有时为了表示某一确切的位置，也用 between 表示 "三者或三者以上的关系"。例如：

Anhui lies *between* Henan, Shandong, Jiangsu, Zhejiang, Jiangxi and Hubei. 安徽位于河南、山东、江苏、浙江、江西和湖北之间。

betwixt

［古、诗、方］，*between*，在…中间，常与 between 连用，构成习语 betwixt and between，意为 "介于两者之间；模棱两可；不全是这样也不全是那样"。例如：

I am forever walking upon these shores, *betwixt* the sand and the foam.
我常常在这些沙滩和大海之间的海岸上漫步。

I trembled all the while *betwixt* fear and hatred.
我又害怕又厌恨，一直在那儿发抖。

He stood *betwixt* two perils. 他进退维谷。

A strange sympathy *betwixt* soul and body!
这是灵魂和肉体之间一种奇妙的共鸣！

That's strange creature; it looks somewhere *betwixt and between* a horse and a dog. 那个动物真奇怪，它看上去既非狗又非马，介于两者之间。

The meal we had at the restaurant was rather *betwixt and between*.
我们在那家餐馆吃的那顿饭不好也不坏。

beyond

(1) *on the far side of; past* 在远处那边；过。例如：

Beyond the mountains is a thick forest. 山那边是一片茂密的森林。

The woods go for about two miles *beyond* the river.
树林在河那边绵延约两英里。

(2) *later than; after* 迟于；在…之后。例如：

Some shops keep open *beyond* midnight. 有些商店营业到半夜以后。

(3) *to a degree that is past the understanding, reach, or scope of* 超出（理解、范围、眼界）之上。例如：

This work is *beyond* my grasp. 这件工作非我力所能及。

This is an evil *beyond* remedy. 这是无可救药的邪恶。

(4) *to a degree or amount greater than* 在程度或数量上大于…。例如：

He lives *beyond* his means. 他入不敷出。

The shares boomed *beyond* the face value. 股票暴涨远远超过了票面价值。

The level of inflation has gone *beyond* 6%. 通货膨胀率已经超过了 6%。

(5) in addition to 除…以外。例如：

I know nothing of it *beyond* what he told me.

除了他告诉我的以外，别的我什么都不知道。

Have you got any other dictionary *beyond* this?

除了这本外，你还有什么别的字典吗？

注：beyond 作"除外"解，通常用于否定句和疑问句，如上例。

but

(1) *except* 除…外，常与 no one, none, nothing 等否定词，who, all, every one 等词或形容词最高级连用。

John is anything *but* honest. 约翰一点不老实。

Who *but* a fool would believe it. 只有傻瓜会相信吧。

They could do nothing *but* wait for the doctor to come. 他们只得等医生来。

This letter is nothing *but* an insult. 这封信完全是一种侮辱。

Most people agreed to my plan *but* you. 大家都赞成我的计划，唯独你反对。

比较：
> We are all present *but/except/save* Smith.
> 除史密斯外我们全到了。
> The gate is never opened *except/save* on Sundays.
> 除了星期天，这大门从来不开。

注：❶ but, except, save 都作"除了…之外（不包括）"解，其后均可跟介词短语或从句，beside 无此用法，save 为古英语用词，属于正式文体。

❷ but 不如 except 语气强。

❸ but 与 except 同义，两者区别在于 except 强调被排除的内容，而 but 强调整体的内容，常修饰表示否定意义的不定代词或疑问代词。例如：

Who *but* Gloria would do such a thing?

除了格洛里亚还有谁愿意干这种事？

❹ 词组 the first/last/next but 往往含有"从…倒数"的意思。例如：

This is the last bus stop *but* one in this street.

这是这条街上倒数第二公共汽车站。

Please look at the last line *but* three. 请看倒数第四行。

He was the last *but* one to arrive. 他是倒数第二个到的。

(2) *without* 通常与 for 连用，意为"要不是"，相当于 "were it not for" 或 "had it not been for"，后跟虚拟语气。例如：

But for my brother's help, I would not have finished.

要不是我兄弟的帮助，我是无法完成的。

by

(1) *near*; *at the side of* 在近处；在旁边。例如：

The school is *by* the river. 学校在河边上。

She was standing *by* the window. 她站在窗户旁边。

The children were playing *by* the river when one of them slipped and fell in.

孩子们在河边玩耍，突然其中一个滑了一跤跌进河里。

(2) *about or on the body of* 在身边，在手头。例如：

Have you got any money *by* you? 你身上带钱了吗？

(3) *by way of*; *via* 经；由；从。例如：

He flew back to New York *by* Paris. 他取道巴黎飞回纽约。

I came here *by* the road along the river. 我是走沿河大道到这里来的。

(4) *near to and then on beyond, often with an implication of disregard or avoidance* 经过…旁边过去，常含有不理睬、避免等意味。例如：

He walked *by* me. 他从我旁边走过。

(5) *not later than, before* 不迟于，在…前。例如：

By tomorrow he'll be here. 他明天就到这儿。

(6) *during* 在···的时候。例如:

The enemy attacked us *by* night. 敌人趁黑夜向我们进攻。

People work *by* day and sleep *by* night. 人们白天工作，夜里睡觉。

注: by 所指的时间，具有持续的意思，和 during 相似，但 by 所指的时间强调该时间所表示的环境和状况，如第一句着重说明敌人借黑夜的掩护向我们进攻；第二句中的 by 表示对照的意思。

(7) *through the agency of* 被; 由，通常用于被动语态。例如:

Hamlet was written *by* Shakespeare.《哈姆雷特》是莎士比亚写的。

注：在某些被动结构中，要用 with 或 to，不用 by。例如:

Love cannot be bought *with* money. 爱情是不能用金钱买的。

She is known *to* all of us as a good dancer.

我们都知道她是一位优秀的舞蹈演员。

(8) *according to* 根据; 按照。例如:

We must play *by* the rules. 我们必须按规则比赛。

Do not judge *by* appearance. 不要以貌取人。

(9) *as regards birth, blood or occupation* 就出身、血统、职业而言。例如:

He is British *by* birth although he was born in France.

他虽然生在法国，但他是英国人。

(10) *in terms of* 按···计算。例如:

Eggs are sold *by* the dozen. 鸡蛋按打出售。

The number of people gathering on the square can be counted *by* the thousands. 聚集在广场的人数能以千计。

(11) *amount, extent, indicating measuration, ratio or degree of excess, inferiority, as in space, time, weight* 等。 计数，界限，通常表示时间、空间、数量等的相差。例如:

His horse won *by* a nose. 他的马以一鼻之差取胜。

China's gross national product increased *by* more than seven percent in 2002. 中国国民生产总值 2002 年增加了百分之七以上。

I am senior to him *by* ten years. 我比他年长十岁。

注: 如果比数置于形容词比较级之前，by 通常省去。例如:

I am *ten years* senior to him. 我比他年长十岁。

I am *three years* older than my sister. 我比我妹妹大三岁。

(12) *by means of* 以…方式，手段。例如：

She earned a living *by* writing. 她靠写作为生。

We went *by* air. 我们乘飞机走。

比较：
{
The houses are lighted *by* electricity.

这些房子是用电照明的。

The houses are lighted *with* electric lights.

这些房子是用电灯照明的。
}

注：by 表示无形的手段，with 表示利用有形的器具。

比较：
{
She struck me *by* the hand. 她打了我的手。

She struck me *with* the hand. 她用手打了我。
}

注：by the hand 指被打者的手，with the hand 指打者的手。

(13) multiplied or divided by 表示相乘（除）（以计算面积）。例如：

This is a room 15 feet *by* 20 feet. 这是一个长 20 英尺，宽 15 英尺的房间。

to divide X *by* Y 用 Y 除 X

(14) *succeeding*; *with succession of* 逐一；连续；累加。例如：

The animals went in 2 *by* 2. 这些动物两个两个地走了进去。

The rain fell from the roof drop *by* drop.

雨水一滴一滴地从屋顶上落下来。

比较：
{
Things go on day *by* day. 事情一天天地过去了。

Day *after* day, she waited for his return.

她日复一日地等待他的归来。
}

注：day by day 表示动作的连续，含有不断重复或每日发生的意味；day after day 表示动作或状态的延续，含有经过的时间久长的意味。

(15) *because of*, *on account of* 由于，因为。例如：

He took the wrong train *by* mistake. 他上错了火车。

He got heart disease *by* smoking too much. 他由于吸烟太多得了心脏病。

(16) *in support of* 支持。例如：

I will stand *by* you in the debate. 辩论中我支持你。

circa

源自拉丁语 circum, *around*, *approximately*; *about*, 意为"近似；大约"，常用于年代前。例如：

He was born *circa* 1060 and died in 1118. 他约生于 1060 年，卒于 1118 年。

This show, featuring the elegant sculpture for which ancient Greece was noted, documented the evolution of naturalism and classicism from *circa* 1000 bc to 500 bc. 这次展出的一大特色是古希腊赖以称著的格调高雅的雕刻，记录了从公元前 1000 年到公元前 500 年自然主义和古典主义的演变过程。

This Black Sea fiddle, a folk instrument from Georgia, Central Europe, (*circa* 1865), is made of wood with inlaid ivory.

这把黑海小提琴来自中欧格鲁吉亚的民间乐器（约公元 1865 年），由镶有象牙的木材制成。

The earliest forms of art in Ireland were prehistoric carved stones (*circa* 2500 bc) that formed parts of megalithic stone monuments and tombs.

爱尔兰艺术的最早形式是石刻（约公元前 2500 年），成为巨石纪念碑和坟墓的一部分。

concerning

about, with regard to, on the subject of 论及，关于。例如：

I spoke to him *concerning* his behavior. 我和他谈了有关他的行为。

Concerning your letter, I am pleased to inform you that you are to receive the order by the end of this week.

关于你的来信，我乐意告诉你，你将在本周末前收到订货。

We'd like to hear what you say *concerning* the matter of packing.

我们很想聆听你们就包装问题发表意见。

The board of directors shall decide all major issues *concerning* the joint venture company. 董事会决定合营公司的一切重大事宜。

They show great anxiety *concerning* their retirement allowance.

他们对自己的养老金问题表示十分焦虑。

注：concerning, regarding, respecting, touching 为 concern, regard, respect, touch 的现在分词，已独立地作为介词使用，是正式书面语言，尤其常用于正式的文件中。为避免造作、僵滞，在一般的语言文字里最好不使用，或尽量少使用这四个介词。

considering

in view of; *taking into consideration* 鉴于；考虑到。例如:

You managed the project well, *considering* your inexperience.

考虑到你缺乏经验，这个方案你已处理得很好了。

Considering his age, the little boy reads very well.

就他的年龄来说，这小男孩读得算挺好的。

The campaign was a great success, *considering* the strong opposition.

就强烈的反对而言，这次竞选运动是巨大的成功。

I think he conducted himself admirably, *considering* the difficult circumstances.

考虑到那种困难的情况，我认为他的表现令人钦佩。

注: ❶ considering 可作连词，后跟从句。例如:

He has done very well, *considering* (that) he has no experience.

考虑到他没有什么经验，他已经干得很不错了。

❷ 口语中，considering 作副词，其后不跟名词或从句，附加在一句话之后，意为 "All things considered"（总的来说，各方面考虑起来）。例如:

We had a good trip, *considering*. 总的来说，我们的旅途还算愉快。

We've not done badly, *considering*. 总的来说，我们干得挺不错的。

Yes, her speed was really quite good, *considering*.

是的，就多方面情况而论，她的速度确实非常快。

counting

由 count 的现在分词转化而来的介词，*including*，表示"包括"之意。例如:

There were four people, or five *counting* the baby. 包括婴儿在内有四五个人。

That makes $70, *counting* the tax. 那能赚 70 美元，包括税款。

There are ten people, not *counting* the guide. 不包括向导，共有十人。

The new monthly average will be about $300, not *counting* overtime.

新的平均月工资水平将大约为 300 美元，不包括加班工资。

cum

源自拉丁语 *kom*, *with*, *combined with*, *along with*, 表示"和，与，连同；附有，

附属；联合；…兼"之意，构成复合词。例如：

a garage -*cum*-workshop 汽车间兼车间

a bed-*cum*-sitting room 寝室兼客厅

a bedroom-*cum*-study 卧室兼书房

an attic-*cum*-studio 阁楼兼画室

vaudeville-*cum*-burlesque 杂耍和滑稽表演

a dwelling-*cum*-workshop 住宅兼工厂

a dining-room-*cum*-study 餐厅兼书房

a policewoman-*cum*-prosecutor 女警察兼起诉人

despite

in spite of, notwithstanding 尽管，不管。例如：

Despite all our efforts we still lost the game.

尽管我们尽了全力，还是输掉了比赛。

Demand for these books is high, *despite* their high price.

尽管这些书价钱昂贵，对它们的需求仍然很高。

Despite a lengthy history of small-scale mining of gems, gold, copper, and coal, systematic exploration of Afghanistan's mineral resources did not begin until the 1960s. 尽管具有小规模开采宝石、金、铜和煤的悠久历史，但阿富汗的矿物资源的系统勘探直到 20 世纪 60 年代才开始。

The continent remains mostly rural, *despite* urban growth in the second half of the 20th century. 尽管在 20 世纪下半叶城市得到了发展，但这个大陆仍然大部分是农村。

注：❶ despite 与 in spite of 同义，但语气比后者要弱。

❷ despite of 和 in despite of 为过时用法，在现代英语中已废止，只用 despite 或 in spite of。

❸ 不要将这两个介词误当成连接词用，若后面要跟从句，必须以 despite/in spite of the fact that 这种表达形式。例如：

They persisted in carrying out the project *despite/in spite of* the fact that it had proved unworkable at the very beginning.

尽管那项计划一开始就证明是不切实际的，但是他们还是坚持要实施。

down

(1) *in a descending direction along*, *upon*, *into*, *or through* 顺沿而下；往下进入；通过…往下。例如：

Nanjing is situated *down* the Yangtze River. 南京位于长江下游。

Our university is farther *down* the expressway.

我们大学就在这条高速公路的前面。

(2) *(of time) throughout* 指时间，（从较远的时期）以来。例如：

The story comes *down* the ages. 这个故事从古代讲到现在。

(3) *from a higher to a lower place* 从…较高到较低处。例如：

She fell *down* stairs. 她从楼梯摔了下去。

(4) *along the course of* 沿。例如：

He was walking *down* the street. 他沿着街走下去。

(5) *in or at* 在…里，在…处。例如：

The cans are stored *down* the cellar. 罐头藏在地窖里。

(6) *from the suburbs to town or downtown areas* (由郊区) 进入市区，(由住宅区) 到商业区；在市区；在商业区。例如：

Let's drive *down* town. 咱们开车到市区去。

She is going *down* town to do some shopping tomorrow. 她明天想进城购物。

during

(1) *throughout the course or duration of* 在…的期间。例如：

They suffered food shortages *during* the war.

他们在战争期间饱受食品短缺之苦。

He fell asleep *during* the lesson. 他在上课时睡着了。

(2) *at some time in* 在…某个时候。例如：

She was born *during* a blizzard. 她生于暴风雪降临的时候。

注：❶ in 和 during 都表示一段时间，凡是能用 in 的地方，一般均可用 during，在这种用法上，during 接近于 in 的意义。例如：

She called on me *during* my absence. 我不在的时候她曾来拜访我。

You shouldn't call on his wife *in* his absence.

他不在的时候你不应去拜访他的妻子。

❷ 但是, during 更强调时间的延续, 而 in 则只是一般地指某一时间。因此, 若谓语动词表示一种状态或习惯性动作, 通常用 during, 否则用 in。此外, 在与 visit, stay, meal 等表示事态延续一定时间的名词搭配时, 只能用 during, 而不能用 in。例如:

During our visit, we learned how to make colored sculptures.

在参观的过程中, 我们也了解了如何制作彩塑。

I came across a few vulgar and vile people *during* my stay.

留居期间, 我遇到了几个粗鄙邪恶的家伙。

The phone rang *during* the meal. 吃饭时电话铃响了。

She was ill for a week, and *during* that week she ate little.

她病了一个星期, 在那一周她吃得很少。

(3) during 与 for 的区别

① during 通常表示事件发生在何时, 而 for 则表示事件持续了多长时间。例如:

He was in hospital for four weeks *during* the summer.

他夏天住了四个星期的医院。

—When did he die? 他是什么时候死的?

—*During* the last war. 是在上次战争中。(此句不能用 for)

—How long did you live there? 你在那儿住过多久?

—*For* about four years. 大约四年。(此句不能用 during)

② 两者之后均可接由 the whole 引起的时间短语, 但通常不能接由 all 引起的时间短语。

比较: { He stayed there *for/during* all the summer. (误)
He stayed there *for/during* the whole summer. (正)
他整个夏天都住在那儿。

③ 在 "数词＋时间名词" 之前以及在 some time, a long time 之类表示泛指一段时间的词组之前, 可用介词 for, 但不用 during。

比较: { He lived here during ten years (during some time). (误)
He lived here for ten years (for some time). (正)
他在这儿住过 10 年 (一段时间)。

ere

previous to, before 在⋯之前，用于诗歌或古体中。例如：

ere the break of day 破晓之前

ere morning 清晨以前

Early on the following morning he commenced the removal of his riches, and *ere* nightfall the whole of his immense wealth was safely deposited in the compartments of the secret locker.

第二天一早，他就开始搬运他的财富，在夜幕落下以前，他那笔庞大的财富已全部安全地藏进了他的秘密柜的暗格里。

注：*ere* 可作连词，意为 "rather than, before"，与其⋯（宁肯）。例如：

the joys that came *ere* I was old 在我未老以前所得的欢乐

I will fight *ere* I will submit. 我宁战不降。

He will die, *ere* he will yield. 他宁死不屈。

Ere you were born was beauty's summer dead.

你们还没有生，美的夏天已死。

ex

(1) 用作介词，限于很狭窄的领域，系股票交易术语，*not including; without*，不包括；没有。例如：

a stock price *ex* dividend 不包括股息的股票价格

ex interest 无利息

ex dividend 不包括下期股息，不计股息

He was willing to buy the shares *ex* rights.

他愿意买进这些无权认购新股的股票。

(2) 商业术语，*free of any transport or handling charges incurred before removal from a given location* 从一特定地点运出之前免收运输或处理的费用。例如：

bought the goods *ex* warehouse 买货物时出仓库前免费

the above price *ex* factory prices, free shipping, offer valid for 1 month

以上价格为工厂交货价格，不含运费，报价有效期在 1 个月内

The goods will be supplied ex stock or *ex* factory at the option of the buyer.

从仓库或直接到工厂提货，由买者选择。

(3) *from, but not having graduated with, the class of* 肄业于···级，出自某一届，但并未同此届毕业生一起毕业。例如：

a Columbia alumnus, *ex* '70 一个出自 70 届的哥伦比亚男肄业生

注：ex 用作前缀，*former* 以前的，前任的。例如：

    ex-convict 从前曾被判刑的人

    ex-president 前任总统

    ex-colony 前殖民地

except

with the exclusion of; other than; but not, not including 除···之外；除外；不包括。例如：

He answered all the questions *except* the last one.

除了最后一个问题外，他回答了所有的问题。

I know nothing about him *except that* he lives next door.

我不了解他的情况，只知道他住在隔壁。

The bus was empty *except for* one old lady.

公共汽车上要不是坐了一位老太太就空了。

注：❶ 关于 except, beside, besides, but 之间的区别，已在 besides 条作了比较，下面再作一些补充说明。

    在现代英语中，but 不可置于句首，except 一般不宜放在句首，放在句首时，应用 except for。例如：

    Except for a forkful of salad, he did not eat a thing.

    除了一叉色拉外，他一样东西都没有吃。

❷ 根据《朗文当代英语辞典》（*Longman Dictionary of Contemporary English*），except for 与 but for 同义，都作 "if it were not for" 解。例如：

    Except for you, I should be dead by now.

    倘若不是因为你，我现在可能死了。

    She would leave her husband *except for* the children.

    若不是因为这些孩子，她就离开她的丈夫了。

❸ except for 后不可直接跟 that 从句，必须采取 except for ＋ the fact ＋ that 这种形式。例如：

I know nothing about his travel *except for the fact that* he will be away for three months. 我对他的旅行一无所知，只知道他将外出三个月。

其实，这种句子很冗大，可以将 for the fact 删去。

excepting

with the exception of 不包括。其意义或多或少与 except 相同，但是在现代英语中，其用法几乎完全局限于否定式 not excepting, 或用于句首，或在 without, always 后面。例如:

All religions, *not excepting* Christianity, run the risk of becoming fossilized.

一切宗教，基督教也不例外，都有变僵化的危险。

Everyone, *not excepting* myself, has the responsibility.

每个人，包括我自己，都有责任。

Everybody must observe the law *not excepting* the president.

人人都必须守法，总统亦无例外。

I think we must keep improving our English *not excepting* those who have mastered it. 我认为我们必须不断提高我们的英语水平，对那些已掌握了英语的人也不例外。

All the people in my family go to work every day, *always excepting* my youngest sister. 我家所有的人每天都上班，除了我那个最小的妹妹以外。

注: excepting 位于句首时，无须同 not, always 或 without 搭配。例如:

Excepting Sundays the stores are open daily.

除了星期天以外，那些商店天天都营业。

Excepting the last chapter, the book is finished.

除了最后一章外，这本书已经完成。

excluding

not counting, leaving out of account 除…外，不包括。例如:

The lunch costs $12 per person, *excluding* drinks.

午餐每人 12 美元，不含饮料。

There were 10 people in the lawyer's office, *excluding* the office boy.

律师事务所里有十个人，不包括勤杂工在内。

The train has sixteen cars, *excluding* the baggage and mail ones.

这列火车，除了行李车和邮车外，有十六节车厢。

Excluding water, half of the body's weight is protein.

除水以外，人体重量的一半是蛋白质。

Excluding these two giants, the developing world would grow only 2.9 percent next year.

剔除这两个大国后，全球发展中国家明年的经济增长率将仅为2.9%。

failing

in the absence or default of, without 因缺少，在缺少…时，没有。例如：

Failing payment, we shall sue. 若不付款，我们将起诉。

Failing instructions I did what I thought was best.

没有任何指示，我只能按我认为最好的方法去做了。

Failing a solution this afternoon, the problem will have to wait until next Monday.

如果今天下午没有解决办法，这个问题将必须等到下周一解决。

Failing agreement on this key issue, the negotiations broke down.

因为在这关键问题上达不成一致，谈判破裂了。

Failing a heavy rainfall soon, the drought will become serious.

如果最近不下一场大雨，旱情将更趋严重。

Failing good weather, the lecture will be held indoors.

如果天气坏，讲演会改在室内举行。

Failing a rainstorm, the game will be played this afternoon.

如果没有暴风雨，今天下午就会玩游戏。

We will probably have the conference at the Hyatt Hotel or, *failing* that, at the Fairmont. 我们很可能在海厄特大酒店举行会议，如果不行，改在费尔蒙特大酒店举行。

following

subsequent to; immediately after (in time) 在…以后；(时间上) 紧跟在…之后。例如：

Following dinner, brandy was served in the study.

正餐后，白兰地酒被端进书房内。

Following the lecture, a discussion was held. 讲座结束后，举行了讨论。

Following the meeting, light refreshments will be served.

会议后将上些易消化的点心。

Following the concert, there will be a champagne reception.

音乐会后，将有香槟酒招待会。

Following the funeral, the family solicitor read the will of the deceased person.

葬礼后，家庭律师宣读了死者的遗嘱。

注：通常情况下，无论哪里有可能，宜优先用 after，而不用 following；然而，有时似乎有些理由用 following（如上例句），因为该词不仅暗示直接性，而且也表示某种联系，因为这两件事均为安排的一部分。

for

（1）*used to indicate the object, aim, or purpose of an action or activity* 为了，用来指一个动作或活动的目的、目标或意图。例如：

He plans to run *for* senator. 他计划竞选参议员。

Time and tide wait *for* no man. 岁月不等人。

注：❶ 一般情况下，英语不用 for doing sth. 来表示目的。例如：

She went there *for* seeing her uncle.（误）

She went there *to* see her uncle. 她去那儿看她叔叔。（正）

❷ 但如果一个动名词已名词化，则可与 for 连用表示目的。例如：

She went there *for* swimming.

她去那儿游泳了。（swimming 已名词化）

❸ 表示原因、用途时，for 可以和动名词连用。例如：

He felt very sorry *for* losing this chance.

失去了这次机会，他怅惘不已。

A voltameter is a scientific instrument used *for* measuring quantity of electricity. 电量计是测量电量的科学仪器。

Sickles and reaping hooks were used *for* cutting the crops.

镰刀和收割钩被用来收庄稼。

（2）*used to indicate a destination* 往，向，用来指目的地。例如：

We set off *for* London. 我们动身去伦敦。

The passenger train is bound *for* Beijing. 这列客车开往北京。

(3) *used to indicate the object of a desire, an intention, or a perception* 对于，用来指愿望、意图或感觉的目标。例如：

She has much talent *for* painting. 她很有绘画才华。

He is eager *for* fame and fortune. 他渴求名利。

比较：$\begin{cases} \text{They searched me/my house.} \\ \text{They searched } \textit{for} \text{ me/} \textit{for} \text{ my house.} \end{cases}$

注：❶ to search a person/house 意为"搜查人的身体 / 家中的东西"；to search for a person/house 意为"搜寻人的行踪，房子的所在地"。

❷ 又如：to send the doctor 意为"派遣医生"，to send for the doctor 意为"派人去请医生"。一词之差，含义不同。

(4) *used to indicate the recipient or beneficiary of an action* 用来表示一个活动的接受者或受益者。例如：

She prepared a big lunch *for* us. 她为我们做了一顿丰盛的午餐。

注：to prepare a feast 意为"设宴"，而 to prepare for the feast 意为"准备赴宴"。同样，to prepare an examination 意为"出或制作考卷"，而 to prepare for the examination 意为"准备参加考试"。

(5) *on behalf of* 代表。例如：

Red is *for* danger. 红色代表危险。

(6) *in favor of* 对…支持。例如：

Were they *for* or against the proposal? 他们支持这项议案还是反对呢？

(7) *in place of* 代替…例如：

Many manufacturers now use plastic as a substitute *for* steel.

现在许多制造厂商用塑料做钢的代用品。

(8) *used to indicate equivalence or equality* 等值，等量，用于表示等值或相同关系。例如：

He paid 50 dollars *for* the book. 他付了 50 美元买这本书。

(9) *used to indicate correlation or correspondence* 用于表示关联或联系。例如：

They took two steps back *for* every step forward.

他们每前进一步向后退两步。

(10) *used to indicate amount, extent, distance, or duration* 用于表示数量、范围、距离或持续时间。例如：

We stayed at the hotel *for* three days. 我们在这家旅馆住了三天。

The Sahara Desert extends *for* thousands of kilometers.

撒哈拉沙漠延绵数千公里。

注：由 for 引导的表示时间、距离的短语，在肯定句中，通常可以省略。但在否定句中，不可省略。例如：

I walked (*for*) ten miles. 我走了十英里路。(句中 for 可省略)

We wondered around the city (*for*) three hours.

我们在城市漫步了三个小时。(句中 for 可省略)

We haven't seen each other *for* ages. 我们好久没见面了。(句中 for 不可省略)

I haven't been there *for* ten years. 我已经有十年没有去那里了。(句中 for 不可省略)

(11) *used to indicate a specific time* 用于表示一个具体时间。例如：

I have an appointment *for* two o'clock. 我两点钟有一个约会。

(12) *as being* 当作。例如：

Don't take everything *for* granted. 不要一切都想当然。

The city girl took wheat *for* leek. 那个城市姑娘把小麦当成了韭菜。

(13) *used to indicate an actual or implied listing or choosing* 针对…用于表示实际的或隐含的列举或选择。例如：

Many people want to buy it because, *for* one thing, the price is low.

许多人想买它，原因之一就是价格便宜。

(14) *as a result of*; *because of* 由于，因为。例如：

Hangzhou is a city famous *for* its beauty.

杭州是一个以风景美丽而著称的城市。

She was praised *for* her excellent work in the company.

她因在公司工作杰出而受到表彰。

(15) *used to indicate appropriateness or suitability* 用于表示适度或适当。例如：

It will be *for* the judge to decide. 这要由法官来决定。

There are a great variety of books *for* children at the bookstore.

这家书店有各种各样的儿童图书。

(16) *notwithstanding*; *despite* 虽然，尽管，常与 all 连用。例如：

For all the problems, it was a valuable experience.

尽管还存在许多问题，这仍不失为一次宝贵的经历。

（17）*as regards*; *concerning* 关于，至于。例如:

I have no ear *for* music. 我对音乐比较外行。

（18）*considering the nature or usual character of* 至于，关于…的性质或一般特征。例如:

He is tall *for* his age. 就他的年龄而言，他是个高个子。

It is warm *for* early February. 对于早春二月来说，天气已经很暖和了。

（19）*in honor of* 为纪念… 例如:

The boy was named *for* his grandmother.

为了纪念他的祖母，人们给这个男孩子起了这个名字。

注: name after 或 name for 都有"向…表示敬意"的意思，美式英语中多用 for。

（20）*corresponding to* 符合，通常前后是一相同的名词，而且该名词前无冠词或修饰语。例如:

Don't translate a passage word *for* word. 不要逐字逐词翻译一篇短文。

（21）*used to indicate recompense, reward, compensation* 用来表示抵偿、赔偿、报酬、报复等义。例如:

What can I pay him *for* his services? 我能做什么来报答他的服务呢?

（22）*used to indicate apology, responsibility* 用来表示道歉、责任等义。例如:

Can you account *for* your absence from the lecture?

你能说明不听讲座的原因吗?

I am responsible *for* my sister until she gets a job.

在我妹妹找到工作以前，我对她负责。

I must apologize *for* calling you so late. 实在抱歉，这么晚给您打电话。

from

（1）*used to indicate a specified place or time as a starting point* 用来表示作为起点的特定地点或时间。例如:

The airport is thirty kilometers *from* the city. 机场离城市有三十公里。

She is fond of reading *from* childhood. 她从小就喜爱读书。

The train goes *from* Paris to Rome. 火车从巴黎开往罗马。

The environment in some countries is going *from* bad to worse.

有些国家的环境状况每况愈下。

(2) *used to express distance or remoteness in space, idea, aim, state etc.* 用来表示场所、思想、目的、情况等的距离、远隔。

This is remote *from* our object. 这绝不是我们的目标。

The story is very distant *from* the truth. 这篇报道离事实太远了。

I am far *from* (being) satisfied with your work.

我对你的工作一点不满意。

(3) *used to indicate a source, a cause, a material, an agent, or an instrument* 用来表示来源、起因、方法或用具。例如:

Bread is made *from* flour. 面包是用面粉做成的。

She is sprung *from* a wealthy family. 她出身于富裕家庭。

I obtained the news *from* a well-informed source.

我从消息灵通人士那里得到这消息。

This temple dates *from* the period of the Three Kingdoms.

这座庙宇始建于三国时代。

(4) *used to indicate separation, removal, or exclusion* 用以表示分离、转移或排除。例如:

We must do what we can to prevent this river *from* being polluted.

我们必须尽一切可能阻止这条河流被污染。

The committee decided to remove him *from* office.

该委员会决定免除他的职务。

注: guard, protect, defend, shelter, shield 等动词后面，常用 against, 但一般而言, against 表示防御、抵抗之意, 而 from 则表示保护安全等意。

(5) *used to indicate differentiation* 用以表示区别。例如:

Can you tell Tom *from* his twin brother?

你能把汤姆和他的孪生兄弟分辨开吗?

Can you separate the good eggs *from* the bad ones?

你能把这些好鸡蛋与坏鸡蛋分开来吗?

(6) *used to show cause or motive; because of* 用来表示原因、动机; 因为, 由于。例如:

He fainted *from* hunger. 他饿昏了。

She was nearly crying *from* the pain of her cut leg.

割破的腿疼痛得使她几乎要哭了。

He did it from his ulterior motive. 他这样做是别有用心。

比较：
> Many people fell ill *from* drinking the muddy water.
> 许多人因喝混浊的水而病倒了。
> It happened *through* his carelessness.
> 那是由于他粗枝大叶造成的。

注: through 表示消极或偶然的原因，而 from 用于自然或直接的原因。

比较：
> The traitor trembled *for* fear. 这个卖国贼因害怕而颤抖。
> The coward obeyed *from* fear. 这个胆小鬼出于惧怕服从了。

注: for fear 表示行为的缘由; from fear 表示动机。

（7）*used to indicate imitation or painting* 用来表示模仿、绘画。例如:

The portrait is drawn *from/after* the life. 这幅肖像是模仿实物绘制的。

（8）*used to indicate inference or conclusion* 用来表示推断、断定。例如:

From what you say I infer that you are not in favor of my proposal.

根据你说的话，我推测你不赞成我的提案。

given

given: *considering*; *taking into account*; *if one has/had*, 意为 "鉴于；考虑到；假如；如果有"，后跟宾语 (不跟副词、副词短语，但可跟从句，作连词)。例如:

Given good weather, our ship will reach Shanghai Monday evening.

假如天气好，我们的船将于星期一晚上到达上海。

Given the general state of his health, it may take him a while to recover from the operation.

考虑到他的健康状况，他可能需要一段时间从手术中恢复过来。

Given her interest in children = Given that she is interested in children, I am sure that teaching is the right career for her.

考虑到她对孩子感兴趣，我可以肯定教书是最适合她的职业。

Given prudence and patience, anybody can achieve something.

如果谨慎和耐心，任何人都可以成就某种事。

gone

gone 由动词 go 演变而来的介词，= *later than*, *past*, 意为 "迟于…，超过…"，非正式英式英语。例如:

It was just *gone* 7 o'clock this evening when I finished.

今晚刚过七点时我就做完了。

It's certainly *gone* 11 o'clock. It must be 11:30.

现在肯定过了 11 点钟，一定到了 11:30。

He's *gone* 50. He must be nearly 60 years old.

他已经年过 50，一定近花甲之年了。

in

（1）*within the limits, bounds, or area of* 在…范围、界限或地区内。例如：

She lives *in* London. 她住在伦敦。

He was standing *in* the room. 他站在房间里。

比较：⎰There are two middle schools *at* that village. 那个村庄有两所中学。
⎱Is there a middle school *in* this village? 这村里有中学吗？

注：在村庄等小地名前面，通常用 at, 但说话的本人在那个村庄里时，应用 in。

比较：⎰She lies *in* a bed.
⎱She lies *on* a bed.

注：to lie in a bed 意为"躺在床上"，指日里的"寝"和 to lie on a bed 也意为"躺在床上"，指夜里的"寝"。

He was hit *in* the face. 他被打中了脸。

比较：⎧Japan is *in* the east of Asia. 日本在亚洲的东部。
⎪Japan lies *to* the east of China. 日本在中国的东方。
⎨Japan faces the Pacific Ocean *on* the east.
⎩日本东临太平洋。

注：❶ in the east 在东部，在范围之内；to the east 在东方，表示在…范围之外；on the east 在东边，在东侧，表示在…范围之外但和它相邻接。

❷ The sun rises *in* the east and sets *in* the west.

日升于东而没于西。句中只能用 in。

（2）*from the outside to a point within; into* 从外面进入；入内。例如：

He threw the letter *in* the wastebasket. 他把信扔进了废纸篓。

注：在 put, cast, split, part, fall, throw, thrust, divide, break 等这类动词后，

可用 in 代替 into。

(3) *to or at a situation or condition of* 达到或处于某种状态或情形。例如:

a woman *in* love 恋爱中的女人

The young beautiful woman was split *in* two in the magical performance.

在魔术表演中，那个年轻美丽的女子被分成两半。

That country in Latin America is now *in* debt.

拉丁美洲那个国家现在债台高筑。

(4) *having the activity, occupation, or function of* 有某种活动、职业或作用。例如:

In his young, he began his life *in* politics. 他年轻时开始政治生涯。

(5) *during the act or process of* 在某行动或过程中。例如:

The volcano is *in* eruption. 火山正在喷发。

The chrysanthemums are *in* flower now. 这些菊花正在盛开。

(6) *with the arrangement or order of* 按照某种安排或秩序。例如:

Novels and stories in a library are arranged *in* alphabetical order according to the author's surname.

图书馆里的小说是根据作者姓氏的字母顺序排列的。

(7) *after the style or form of* 以某种风格或形式。例如:

Her composition is written *in* prose. 她的作文是用散文体写的。

Moment in Peking by Lin Yutang was written *in* English.

林语堂的《京华烟云》是用英文写的。

(8) *with the characteristic, attribute, or property of* 具有某种特征、品质或属性，如品质、性格、能力、性质、行为、思想、身份、穿戴等。例如:

She has something of the artist *in* her. 她有艺术家的气质。

He was a tall man *in* an overcoat. 他是个穿着大衣的高大男人。

In my opinion you are mistaken. 我认为你错了。

比较: { I do not believe him.
       I do not believe *in* him.

注: to believe someone 相信某人的话 (to accept one's statement as true); to believe in someone 相信某人诚实，有能力等 (to trust in one's honesty, capacity)。

(9) *by means of* 以某种方式。例如：

She paid for the computer *in* cash. 她用现金买了这台电脑。

China is now developing its Northwest *in* a big way.

中国正在大规模地开发大西北。

The telegram was dispatched *in* cipher code. 这封电报是用密码发送的。

(10) *used to indicate time* 用来表示时间。

① *within the limits of a period* 在…时间、时期内。例如：

The People's Republic of China was founded *in* the year 1949.

中华人民共和国成立于 1949 年。

There were two world wars *in* the last century.

20 世纪发生过两次世界大战。

② *within the space of time* 在…期间内。例如：

He finished the work *in* two days. 他在两日内完成了那项工作。

She will write another novel *in* two years.

她将在两年内写出另一部小说。

③ *in the course of* 在…（时间）后，过…（时间），多用于一般将来时。

例如：

I'll be back *in* half an hour. 我将在半小时后回来。

The project will be completed *in* six months.

这项工程将在六个月后完成。

比较：
⎧ She will return *in/within* a week's time.
⎪ 她将在一星期后 / 内回来。
⎨ The sun will not rise *for* an hour.
⎩ 过一小时太阳将升起。

注：❶ in 表示将来某时期的完结（at the close of some future period），
within 表示不到某时期完结（in a time no longer than）。

❷ for 用在否定句中，表示将来的一时期，但如在肯定句中，必
须用 in。

❸ for 表示一段时间，用于肯定句时，可以省略，但在否定句中
不可省略。例如：

I'm sorry to have kept you waiting (*for*) a long time.

对不起，让你久等了。

I haven't seen you *for* ages. 好久未见到你了。

(11) *made with or through the medium of* 用或通过某种媒介。例如：

This is a statue *in* bronze. 这是一尊青铜雕像。

(12) *with the aim or purpose of* 有某种目的或目标。例如：

The policeman followed *in* pursuit. 那警察在跟踪。

A feast will be given tomorrow *in* his honor. 明天将为他举行欢迎宴会。

(13) *with reference to* 关于。例如：

I have faith *in* your judgment. 我确信你的判断。

China is rich *in* natural resources. 中国矿物资源丰富。

He is a scientist *in* name, but not *in* fact. 他是个有名无实的科学家。

(14) *used to indicate price, amount, number, rate, ratio or proportion* 用于指价格、数量、数目、比率，比例等。例如：

In recent years college students are enrolled *in* ever-increasing numbers.

近年来，大学生入学人数在日益增加。

Volume is *in* inverse proportion to pressure. 体积和压力成反比。

Pupils go to school *in* twos and threes. 学生们三三两两地去上学。

He pays the balance *in* one sum. 他把余额一笔付清了。

The box is six inches *in* depth. 盒子的深度为六英寸。

including

实为现在分词，不过在许多上下文中起到介词作用，意为 "not omitting, counting within or amongst, having as a part of a whole, containing"，不遗漏，计入，整体的一部分，包括。例如：

Seven were killed, *including* the guide. 包括向导在内，共七人丧生。

The terrorists wanted everyone as hostages, *including* the children.

这些恐怖分子想把所有人劫为人质，包括儿童。

He had several injuries, *including* three fractures.

他多处受伤，其中三处骨折。

He has many occupations *including* gardening and wine-making.

他有许多消遣，包括园艺和酿酒。

A new car of this kind costs $8,000, *including* purchase tax.

这种新车要价 8000 美元，包括购买税。

注: including 及其宾语有时可以置于句首。例如:

Including the servants, there were twelve people in the house.

包括佣人在内，房内共有12人。

inside

(1) *within* 在…以内，表示地点或时间。例如:

She was standing just *inside* the gate. 她恰恰站在大门里面。

She put the money *inside* her bag. 她把钱放在包里。

We'll be there *inside* an hour. 我们一个小时内到达那里。

注: inside 表示时间是美国用法，意思和 within 相同，主要用于口语。
inside 后面的 of 可以省略。

下面摘自《美国传统辞典》(*American Heritage Dictionary*) 的一句话:

The construction *inside of* has sometimes been criticized as redundant or colloquial. But *inside of* is well established in formal writing, particularly in reference to periods of time. (*inside of* 的结构有时被斥为冗长的或口语化的，但 *inside of* 在正式书面语中，特别是用来指时间阶段时，已得到确认。) 例如:

They usually return the manuscript *inside of* (*or inside*) a month.

他们通常在一个月内归还手稿。

(2) *on the inner side or part of* 在内侧或内部。例如:

The necklace was put *inside* the package. 项链放在包裹里面。

(3) *into the interior of* 进入里面。例如:

Many mosquitoes flew *inside/into* the house. 许多蚊子飞进了屋里。

注: into 仅表示由外向内进入；inside 常指与外部相接的最内部。此外，inside 作"到…里面"解时，多半指进入某一界限的里面，如 to step inside the gate 踏进大门内，to jump inside the window 跳进窗户内。但有时也指进入一个空间，如上句。在这种情况下，inside 的意思与 into 相同，可以互用。

into

(1) *to the inside or interior of* 到…的里面或内部。例如:

The sun was shining full *into* her room. 阳光洒满了她的房间。

(2) *to the activity or occupation of* 从事…的活动或职业。例如：

They are recent college graduates who go *into* banking.

他们是从事金融业的应届大学毕业生。

He was assigned to look *into* the case. 他被委派去调查这宗案件。

(3) *to the condition, state, or form of* 转为…的条件，状态或形式。例如：

The dishes broke *into* pieces. 碟子摔成了碎片。

The two young lovers changed *into* a pair of butterflies.

这两个年轻的恋人变成了一对蝴蝶。

(4) *so as to be in or be included in* 以便在…里面，或被包括在…里面。例如：

These parties entered *into* an agreement. 这些党派达成了一项协议。

She wrote a new character *into* the play. 她在该剧中加入了一个新角色。

(5) *interested in or involved with* 对…感兴趣，卷入。例如：

They are *into* vegetarianism. 他们对素食主义感兴趣。

(6) *to a point within the limits of a period of time or extent of space* 到一段时间范围，或一定空间范围内的程度。例如：

We danced folk dances far *into* the night.

我们跳起了民间舞蹈，一直跳到深夜。

(7) *in the direction of; toward* 朝在…方向；向。例如：

She looked *into* the distance. 她向远处望去。

The spire pointed *into* the blue sky. 塔尖指向蓝天。

(8) *against* 触及；碰靠在。例如：

The car crashed *into* a tree. 那辆小汽车撞到了一棵树上。

(9) *as a divisor of* 除，作为…的除数。例如：

The number 3 goes *into* 9 three times. 9 除 3 等于 3。

(10) *forming a part of* 形成…的一部分。例如：

Financial matters entered *into* the discussion. 财政问题被纳入讨论之列。

(11) *expressing the result brought out by some action* 表示动作的结果。常与 talk, frighten, reason, drive, argue, bribe, deceive, worry, strike, coax, trick, force, persuade, shock 等动词连用。例如：

Who persuaded you *into* writing the letter? 谁劝你写的那封信？

The bombing attack struck fear *into* their hearts. 轰炸使他们心惊肉跳。

less

with the deduction of; *minus* 减去；差，其反义词为 plus。例如：

fifty pounds *less* income tax 50 英镑减去所得税

eight ounces *less* the weight of the container 8 盎司减去容器重量

eight hundred pounds, *less* commission at 2.5% 800 英镑，扣去 2.5% 佣金

a year *less* two days 一年差两天

Five *less* two is three. 5 减 2 等于 3。

She gave me £100, *less* £20 for her own costs.

她给我 100 英镑，扣去她花了的 20 英镑。

like

(1) *possessing the characteristics of*; *resembling closely*; *similar to* 具有…的特点；相像；相似。例如：

The flower was something *like* a large daisy. 这花有点像一枝大雏菊。

The child is *like* its mother in looks. 这小孩外貌像他母亲。

Your necklace is *like* mine. 你的项链和我的很像。

There is nothing *like* a cold drink of water when one is thirsty.

人渴时，没有什么东西像一杯冰水那样解渴。

(2) *in the typical manner of* 以…的典型方式。例如：

It's not *like* you to take offense. 你不像会发脾气的人。

It would be *like* him to forget our appointment. 他好像忘记了我们的约会。

(3) *in the same way as* 以与…同样的方式。例如：

He lived *like* royalty. 他过着帝王般的生活。

He ran *like* hell. 他拼命地跑。

He dresses *like* his brother. 他的服饰与他哥哥的相似。

(4) *inclined or disposed to* 想要，倾向，有意于。例如：

Do you feel *like* a walk? 你想去散散步吗？

I feel *like* going to bed. 我想睡觉了。

(5) *as if the probability exists for* 像要，似有…的可能性。例如：

It looks *like* a rich year for farmers. 对农民来说，看起来像丰收年。

It looks *like* rain. 天看起来像要下雨。

(6) *such as*; *for example* 诸如。例如：

I want to do something really different, *like* skydiving.

我想做点的确与众不同的事，比如跳伞运动。

There are numerous hobbies you might enjoy, *like* photography or painting.

有许多你也许喜欢的爱好，如摄影或绘画。

mid

surrounded by; *amid* 被…包围的；在…中间的。用于诗歌，与 *amid* 同义，参见 *amid*。例如：

mid smoke and flame 在烟火之中

Reality is the unity of harmony *mid* the conflict.

现实社会是冲突与和谐的统一体。

midst

among, *amid* 在…中间。midst 常用作名词，作介词主见于诗歌，与 *amidst* 同义，参见 *amidst*。例如：

He rode down the street *midst* the cheers. 他在欢呼声中沿街骑马而行。

minus

(1) *reduced by the subtraction of*; *less* 减去，差。例如：

Nine *minus* three is six. 9 减 3 等于 6。

Just as individuals report their incomes, corporations must report gross profits, the year's total sales *minus* the costs of production.

正如个人必须申报其收入一样，公司也必须申报毛利润，年总销售额，减去生产成本。

Natural increase (the birthrate *minus* the death rate, without regard for the effects of migration) is averaging slightly fewer than 140,000 persons a month. 自然增长（出生率减去死亡率，不考虑移民影响）每月平均略低于 140,000 人。

(2) *without*, *lacking* 无，缺少，用于口语。例如：

a book *minus* its title page 一本没有扉页的书

I went to work *minus* my briefcase.

我在没有公文包的情况下去上班。

They returned *minus* their dog. 他们回来了，少了他们的狗。

He came back *minus* his pocketbook. 他回家时身上少了皮夹。

(3) *below zero* 在零以下。例如:

The temperature is *minus* 20 degrees. 温度是零下 20 度。

near

(1) *to express proximity or vicinity in space*, 表示在空间···附近、临近。例如:

He lives in a house *near* the park. 他住在公园附近的一间房子里。

She knew she was *near* the shore because the light was high up on the cliffs.
她知道已接近海岸了，因为灯是高挂在悬崖上的。

(2) *to convey the idea of closeness or approach to, in space, time, or age* 表示在
空间、时间、年龄上临近或接近之意。例如:

The small child was afraid to *go near* the dog. 那小孩不敢靠近那只狗。

He never goes *near* a public house. 他从不去酒馆。

It was *near* midnight we got back home. 我们回到家时已午夜了。

He must be getting *near* retiring age. 他一定快到了退休年龄。

He is *near* forty. 他年近四十。

(3) *to or at a short distance from* (*in condition, state, or resemblance*) (在条件、
状态、相似性方面) 接近，不远。例如:

We are *near* success. 我们要成功了。

Nothing ancient or modern seems to come *near* it.
古今一切似乎没有一种事可与之相比。

(4) 后接形容词或分词表示该形容词或分词所表达的意思, near 前常有
nowhere, anywhere, somewhere 等。例如 :

Your answer is nowhere *near* right. 你的回答完全不对。

The work is nowhere *near* finished yet. 这项工作还远远没有完成。

The cinema was nowhere *near* full. 电影院离满座还差得远呢。

nearby

near, close to, next to 在···附近。例如:

They will build a pumping station *nearby* the bridge.

他们将要在桥附近建造一个抽水站。

We're going to build a new school *nearby* the station.

我们打算在车站附近修建一所学校。

注：nearby 常作副词或形容词，偶尔作介词。例如：

Nearby was a factory which exuded a pungent smell.

附近有一家散发出一股刺鼻气味的工厂。

It happened that there was a telephone booth *nearby*.

碰巧附近有个公用电话亭。

He usually trades at the *nearby* supermarket.

他通常在附近的超市购物。

neath

[古、诗、方]，为 beneath 之缩写，意为"在…之下"。例如：

Go to sleep, now, dear love, *neath* roses above.

好了，亲爱的，去睡吧，就在上面的玫瑰下睡吧。

Deep *neath* the image lies my secret. 在这尊塑像深处下存放着我的秘密。

There *'neath* the flowers of Life ever living, searched I the hearts and the secrets of men. 在那永存的生命之花下面，我搜寻着人类的情感和秘密。

next

adjacent to 邻近的，靠近…的，毗连…的。例如：

Our house stands *next* the church. 我们的房子离教堂很近。

The girl sitting *next* me talked rough. 坐在我旁边的女孩说话很粗鲁。

The emergency brake is located *next* the the gearshift.

紧急制动器在变速器的旁边。

注：在 next to 中，next 为副词，与 next 同义，但还含有"在顺序或程度上接着的"，"几乎，实际上"的意思。例如：

The second night she sat *next to* me. 第二天晚上，她坐到了我的旁边。

May I bring my chair *next to* yours? 我可以把我的椅子移到你的旁边吗？

She ate *next to* nothing at dinner. 晚饭时她几乎什么也没吃。

It is *next to* impossible to cure her illness. 要治好她的病几乎是不可能的。

nigh

not far from; *near* 近的，不远的；靠近的。例如：

None may come *nigh* them. 没有人可以走近他们。

The well was *nigh* the house. 这口井离屋子很近。

She stood *nigh* me. 她站在我旁边。

注: nigh 可作形容词，*being near* (*in time, place, or relationship*) (在时间、地点、关系方面) "接近的"；作副词时，常与 on, upon, about, onto 连用，nearly; almost，"接近；几乎"。例如：

Evening draws *nigh*. 夜晚就要到了。

We talked for *nigh* onto two hours. 我们谈了近两个小时。

He was *nigh* upon 20 miles. 他离家差不多有20英里。

It is well *nigh* impossible to convince him. 要说服他几乎不可能。

Chilly gusts of wind with a taste of rain in them had well *nigh* depeopled the streets. 阵阵寒风夹着零星雨点已使街上几乎空无一人了。

notwithstanding

despite, in spite of 尽管，虽然。例如：

He came *notwithstanding* the rain. 尽管下雨他仍来了。

Notwithstanding his objections the marriage took place.

尽管他有异议，婚礼还是进行了。

I love the boy *notwithstanding* his naughtiness.

尽管这男孩顽皮，但我仍然喜欢他。

注: ❶ *notwithstanding* ＋ that 构成复合连词，引导让步状语从句，表示"虽然，尽管"之意，省去 that, *notwithstanding* 就是连词，现已罕用。例如：

She went swimming yesterday *notwithstanding* (*that*) her mother told her not to. 虽然她妈妈告诉不要去游泳，但她昨天还是去了。

❷ *notwithstanding* 有时置于名词短语之后，意思不变。例如：

Language difficulties *notwithstanding*, he soon grew to love the country and its people.

虽然言语不通，他还是很快就爱上了这个国家及该国人民。

of

(1) *derived or coming from*; *originating at or from* 从…产生；来自…；源于或来自。例如：

I demanded an immediate reply *of* him. 我要求他立即答复。

May I ask a question *of* you? 我可以请教你一个问题吗？

注：上两句中的 of 与 from 同义，可以通用。类似的动词还有 learn, obtain, buy, borrow, hire, hold, want, receive, expect, win, require 等。

(2) *caused by*; *resulting from* 由…引起；由…而致。例如：

Your illness comes *of* eating too much. 你生病的原因是吃得太多。

He died *of* tuberculosis. 他死于肺结核。

He offered help *of* his own accord. 他自愿给予帮助。

I did it *of* necessity, not *of* choice. 我做那件事是根据需要而不是出于选择。

What has become *of* her? 她的情况怎么样了？

注：上句的 to become of 通常用在 what 后面，表示人或事物的结果、境况等。

(3) *away from*; *at a distance from* 离…；距…；差…。例如：

The Chaohu Lake is about 50 kilometers south *of* Hefei.
巢湖在合肥南约50公里。

I came to Beijing within a week *of* his arrival.
在他到达后的一周内，我来到了北京。

It is five minutes *of* five. 差五分五点。

注：上句是美国说钟点的一种方法。在英式英语用 to, 用 to 在美式英语也很普遍。

(4) *so as to be separated or relieved from* 为了分开，从…中解脱；表示"由…分离、脱离、免除、接触、消除、剥夺、治愈"等义。例如：

Tsarist Russia robbed China *of* vast areas of territory.
沙俄从中国掠夺了大片领土。

This medicine will cure you *of* your disease. 这种药将治好你的病。

Computers are relieving office staff *of* their daily chores.
计算机正在把办公室工作人员从日常繁琐事务中解脱出来。

Developed countries should free some very poor countries in the Third World *of* their debts. 发达国家应该免除第三世界一些十分贫穷国家的债务。

The furniture is clean *of* dust. 家具上清洁无尘。

We have to rid the house *of* the mice. 我们必须除掉屋内的老鼠。

注：以上各句中的 of, 常与某些动词搭配，如: cheat, defraud（骗取、诈取）rid, cure, rob, relieve, deliver, absolve（免除），free, plunder（掠夺，抢劫），purge（清除、清洗）等；也可以和某些形容词搭配，如: free, independent, clear, clean, quit, void（空的、没有、缺乏），bare, empty, devoid（缺乏的、空的、无的）等。

比较：{ He is *free from* blame. 他是无可责怪的。
{ This article is *free of* duty. 这件物品免税。

注：❶ free from 没有，用在无过失，无嫌疑，无责任，无缺点，无危险，无忧愁，无痛苦等场合；free of 指被允许的，用在免费，免租，免债，免税，免息，免试等场合。

❷ of 表示"分离"、"免除"等意思，是从其表示根源的原意转用而来的，表示从一种事物或状态里分离或解除出来，因此有时可以和 from 互换使用。例如:

The summit is clear *from* obstructions to the sight.

峰峦毕现，一览无遗。

The roads are clear *of* traffic. 道路畅通无阻。

(5) *from the total or group comprising* 从总体或组成中离开的，表示部分与全体的关系。

① 用在数词或表示数量等意义的名词、代词、形容词后面。例如:

I bought the dress at one-half *of* the usual price.

我以平时一半的价格买了那件衣服。

He has seen much/little *of* life. 他见过很多 / 很少世面。

She is a friend *of* mine (= one *of* my friends). 她是我的一个朋友。

② 用在表示种类、性质等义的名词后面。例如:

Honesty is a species *of* virtue. 诚实是一种美德。

He has a sort *of* wisdom. 他有某种智慧。

③ 用在比较级或含有最高级意味的形容词、副词、名词等后面。例如:

Hydrogen is the lightest *of* all elements. 氢是所有元素中最轻的。

It is unimaginable that you, *of* all people, should do such a thing.

偏偏是你干了这么一件事，真是不可想象。

He is the hero *of* heroes. 他是最杰出的英雄。

Tom is the cleverer *of* the two boys. 汤姆是两个男孩中比较聪明的一个。

④ 和动词连用，如：partake, give, eat, smell, taste, breathe 等，表示分享、给予、吃喝、嗅、尝、呼吸等一部分或具有某种性质或特征等意义。例如：

The guests partook *of* a delicious dinner. 客人们分享了一顿美味的晚餐。

The garden smells *of* sweet roses. 这花园散发着玫瑰的清香。

It tastes *of* lemon. 这东西有柠檬味道。

(6) *composed or made from* 由…组成，由…制成。例如：

This is a dress *of* silk. 这是一件丝制的衣服。

The house is built *of* steel and concrete. 这所房子是用钢筋混凝土建的。

(7) *associated with or adhering to* 与…相接。例如：

He is a man *of* your religion. 他是和你宗教信仰相同的人。

(8) *belonging or connected to* 属于的，与…相连。例如：

He is *of* a clinging sort. 他是那种要依靠人家的人。

William Shakespeare was the greatest playwright *of* his day.

威廉·莎士比亚是他那个时代最伟大的剧作家。

(9) *possessing*; *having* 占有的；拥有的。例如：

He is a person *of* reputation. 他是个有声望的人。

(10) *on one's part* 在某人一方，引出不定式的逻辑主语。例如：

It's very nice *of* you to come to see me. 你来看望我真好。

(11) *containing or carrying* 包含的或含有的。例如：

I am going to buy a bag *of* potatoes. 我打算去买一袋土豆。

She got a basket *of* groceries at the store.

她在那家商店买了一篮子食品杂货。

(12) *specified as*; *named or called* 具体为；被称为，叫作。例如：

a depth *of* ten feet 十英尺的深度

the Garden *of* Eden 伊甸园

(13) *centering on*; *directed toward* 以…为中心的；指向…的，表示动宾关系。例如：

He developed a love *of* literature. 他培养了对文学的爱好。

(14) *produced by*; *issuing from* 由…产生；出自… 例如：

We are satisfied with the results *of* the experiment.

我们对实验的结果感到满意。

(15) *characterized by* 以…为特征的。例如：

They experienced a year *of* famine. 他们经历了饥荒年。

(16) *with reference to*; *about* 关于。例如：

We thought highly *of* her proposals. 我们对她的提议评价很高。

(17) *in respect to* 就…来说。例如：

She is slow *of* speech. 她讲话很慢。

She is quick *of* eye. 她眼光敏锐。

(18) *set aside for*; *taken up by* 为…而设置；由…占据。例如：

She will have a day *of* rest the day after tomorrow. 她后天休息一天。

(19) *during or on a specified time* 在某一规定的期间或时间内。例如：

She has done a lot of reading *of* late. 她最近读了很多书。

He often goes to the library *of* a Sunday. 星期日他常到图书馆去。

She would read aloud in the classroom *of* a morning.

早晨她往往在教室里高声朗读。

注：上两句中的 of a/an…（时间）表示行为惯常地在此时间发生或进行。

句中的 of a Sunday 和 of a morning 与 on Sundays 和 in the mornings

同义，但这种表达方式现在已少见了。

(20) *by* 被。被动语态的施动者的表现形式之一。例如：

The grandfather is beloved *of* the family. 这位祖父被全家人所爱戴。

(21) *used to indicate an appositive* 用来表示同位语。例如：

My sister works in the city *of* Xi'an. 我的妹妹在西安市工作。

He is that idiot *of* a driver. 他就是那个白痴司机。

(22) *used with two nouns, when the first is descriptive of the second* 与两个名词

连用，前者描述后者。例如：

a fine figure *of* a woman 体态匀称的女子

This crampfish *of* a Socrates has so bewitched him.

这条电鱼般的苏格拉底就这样迷住了他。

(23) *used with noun and gerund, being equivalent to an infinitive* 与名词和动名

词连用，相当于动词不定式。例如：

Few people take the trouble *of* finding out what democracy really is.

很少有人不怕麻烦地去弄清真正的民主是什么。（of finding = to find）

off

(1) *removed or distant from* 离开或远离。例如：

The bird hopped *off* the branch. 那只鸟跳离枝条。

Keep *off* the grass. 勿践踏草坪。

(2) *away or relieved from* 离开，从…解脱开。例如：

He is *off* smoking. 他戒烟了。

You are going *off* the subject. 你离题了。

He is *off* duty. 他下班了。

(3) *by consuming* 以…为食。例如：

These birds live *off* locusts and honey. 这些鸟以吃蝗虫和蜂蜜为生。

(4) *with the means provided by* 由…提供的方式。例如：

Many old people live *off* their pensions. 许多老人靠他们的养老金为生。

(5) *from, indicating source* 从…来，表示来源。例如：

What else do you want *off* me? 你还想从我这儿得到些什么？

I bought the dictionary *off* him. 我从他那里买了这本字典。

(6) *extending or branching out from* 从…扩充或分支出来的。例如：

This is an artery *off* the heart. 这是从心脏分支出的一条动脉。

(7) *not up to the usual standard of* 没有达到通常水准的。例如：

He was *off* his game. 他竞技状态不佳。

(8) *so as to abstain from* 为了戒除的。例如：

She went *off* narcotics. 她因麻醉而昏睡过去。

(9) *of, indicating material or substance* 表示材料、物质。例如：

She made a meal *off* fish. 她用鱼做了一顿饭。

(10) *from by subtraction or deduction* 减去，扣除。例如：

He is two years *off* sixty. 他差两岁就六十岁了。

She took ten percent *off* the price. 她减价了百分之十。

(11) *deviating from something normal or usual* 失常，越轨。例如：

She looks rather *off* color. 她的气色看上去不好。

He threw himself *off* balance. 他失去了平衡。

(12) *to seaward of* 向海的方向的，离开海岸的。例如：

Our ship is now a mile *off* the port of Ningbo.

我们的轮船现在距宁波港一英里。

His family is on an island *off* the coast of the southeast.

他家在东南沿海的一个岛屿上。

on

(1) *used to indicate position above and supported by or in contact with* 在…上，被…支撑，与…接触的位置。例如：

The vase is *on* the table. 花瓶在桌子上。

We rested *on* our hands and knees. 我们把头靠在手和膝盖上休息。

(2) *used to indicate contact with or extent over* (*a surface*) *regardless of position* 在…上面，表示不考虑位置接触或在某一表面上。例如：

We put up a picture *on* the wall. 我们在墙上挂了一幅画。

There was a rash *on* my back. 我背上长了疹子。

(3) *used to indicate location at or along* 用以表示…位置或沿着… 例如：

The pasture *on* the south side of the river came into our view.

河岸南边的牧场映入我们的眼帘。

We saw rows upon rows of houses *on* the highways.

我们看到了高速公路边鳞次栉比的房子。

(4) *used to indicate proximity* 表示接近。例如：

I, along with a group of tourists, visited a town *on* the border.

我和一群游客参观了靠近边界的一个市镇。

(5) *used to indicate attachment to or suspension from* 表示附在…上，或悬于…上。例如：

The monks were counting out beads *on* the strings.

和尚们在数细绳上的念珠。

(6) *used to indicate figurative or abstract position* 用以表示比喻的或抽象的位置。例如：

The woman manager is *on* the young side, but experienced.

这个女经理相当年轻，但经验丰富。

He is *on* the sly. 他很狡猾。

(7) *used to indicate actual motion toward, against, or onto* 用于表示实际的动作朝向⋯，对着⋯，在⋯上。例如：

Martin Luther King and other black leaders organized the 1963 March *on* Washington, a massive protest in Washington, D.C., for jobs and civil rights. 马丁·路德·金和其他黑人领袖组织了 1963 年向华盛顿的进军，在首都华盛顿为争取工作和权利的大规模抗议活动。

(8) *used to indicate figurative or abstract motion toward, against, or onto* 用于表示比喻或抽象的运动，朝向⋯，对着⋯，或在⋯之上。例如：

It was going *on* six o'clock. 快到六点了。

He came *on* the answer by accident. 他偶然找到了答案。

(9) *used to indicate occurrence at a given time* 用于表示某一时间事件的发生，特殊时日。例如：

The United States of America was founded *on* July 4, 1776. 美利坚合众国成立于 1776 年 7 月 4 日。

(10) *used to indicate the particular occasion or circumstance* 用以表示某一特定场合或情况；"一⋯就"，可与 upon 换用，接名词或动名词。例如：

On entering the room, she saw him. 她一进这个房间便看到了他。

(11) *used to indicate the object affected by actual, perceptible action* 用于表示实际的、能察觉到的行为影响到的目标。例如：

All at once, the spotlight fell *on* the actress. 聚光灯突然把光集中打到女演员身上。

She knocked gently *on* the door. 她轻轻地敲了门。

(12) *used to indicate the object affected by a figurative action* 用于表示一个比喻影响到的目标。例如：

She had pity *on* the homeless child on the road and took him home. 她很同情这个路边无家可归的孩子，并把他带回了家。

(13) *used to indicate the object of an action directed, tending, or moving against it* 用于表示一动作目标，指向、朝向或移向。例如：

The rebels started an attack *on* the fortress. 反叛者对城堡开始发起攻击。

(14) *used to indicate the object of perception or thought* 用于表示感觉或思考的对象。例如：

Never in his life had he gazed *on* such beautiful scenes.

他生平从未见过如此美丽的景色。

He was meditating *on* the meaning of life. 他在思考人生的意义。

(15) *used to indicate the agent or agency of a specified action* 用于表示对某一特定行为的媒介和工具。例如：

He cut his foot *on* the broken glass. 碎玻璃把他的脚扎破了。

Mr Smith is *on* the telephone now. 史密斯先生正在打电话。

(16) *used to indicate a medicine or other corrective taken or undertaken routinely* 用于表示经常性服用的药物或矫正性行为。例如：

She goes *on* a strict diet. 她实行严格的节食。

(17) *used to indicate a substance that is the cause of an addiction, a habit, or an altered state of consciousness* 用于表示引起上瘾、习惯或意识状态改变的某种物质。例如：

She was high *on* marijuana. 她沉醉于大麻烟中。

(18) *used to indicate a source or basis* 用于表示来源或基础。例如：

We will reach our judgments not *on* intentions or *on* promises but *on* deeds and *on* results. 我们将根据行为和结果而不是意图或诺言来作出判断。

He was arrested *on* suspicion. 他因有嫌疑而被捕。

(19) *used to indicate the state or process of* 用来表示…的状态或过程；从事…例如：

The family went *on* holiday last week. 这家人上星期度假去了。

He is *on* a visit to Europe. 他正在访问欧洲。

(20) *used to indicate the purpose of* 用来表示意图、目的。例如：

He runs *on* errands in the company. 他在这家公司跑腿办差事。

No admittance except *on* business. 非公莫入，闲人免进。

(21) *used to indicate a means of conveyance* 用来表示运送方式、工具。例如：

She goes to work *on* a minibus every day. 她每天乘小公共汽车上班。

(22) *used to indicate availability by means of* 用来表示利用…方式获取。例如：

Doctors are expected to be *on* call day and night. 医生们应日夜随叫随到。

(23) *used to indicate belonging to or a member of* 用来表示"归属…"，"是…的成员"。例如：

He is *on* the editorial department of China Daily.

他是《中国日报》编辑部的一名编辑。

He is now *on* the football team of the university.

他现在是该大学足球队的一名队员。

(24) *used to indicate addition or repetition* 用来表示累加或重复。例如：

He incurred loss *on* loss in his business last year.

去年他的生意屡屡蒙受损失。

(25) *concerning*; *about* 涉及；关于。例如：

I like to read books *on* computers. 我喜欢读关于计算机的书籍。

(26) *concerning and to the disadvantage of* 关于且不利于。例如：

We have some evidence *on* him. 我们有一些不利于他的证据。

(27) *in one's possession, with or on the body of* 拥有；随身带着。例如：

I haven't a cent *on* me. 我一分钱都没带。

(28) *having as a standard, confirmation, or guarantee* 作为标准、确认或保障。例如：

I had it *on* good authority. 我是通过正常途径获得的。

On my word, he is innocent. 我发誓，他是无辜的。

(29) *at the expense of*; *compliments of* 以…为代价；称赞。例如：

The drinks are *on* me. 我请大家喝酒。

onto

(1) *on top of*; *to a position on*; *upon* 在…之上；在…顶端；在一位置上；在…上面。例如：

The dog jumped *onto* the chair. 这条狗跳到了椅子上面。

My cat just jumped *onto* the keyboard. 我的猫刚刚跳到键盘上了。

She has got *onto* the right track in her teaching. 她的教学已上正道。

I reached the gate that opened *onto* the lake. 我走到临湖而开的那扇门前。

(2) *(informal) fully aware of*; *informed about* (非正式用语) 知晓，非常熟悉；了解。例如：

The police are *onto* the robbers' plans. 警察局都清楚抢劫犯的阴谋。

I'm *onto* your scheme. 我了解你的计谋。

注：❶ onto 有时拼作两个单词，尤其在英式英语中。例如：

The dog jumped *on to* the chair. 这条狗跳到了椅子上面。

❷ 小品词 on ＋介词 to 总是写成两个单词。例如:

From Lancaster we went *on to* York.

离开了兰开斯特，我们接着去约克。

❸ 当 on 为动词不定式的一部分时，必须写成两个单词。例如:

He went *on to* tell us his experience in New York.

他接着告诉我们他在纽约的经历。

opposite

(1) *across from, facing* 在…对面，面对。例如:

She parked the car *opposite* the bank. 她将车停在银行对面。

He lives *opposite* the pub. 他住在酒店的对面。

South is *opposite* north on a compass. 罗盘上南与北是相对的。

I glanced at the person who sat *opposite* me.

我向坐在我对面的那个人瞥了一眼。

(2) *in a complementary role to* 演对手戏。例如:

He played *opposite* Marilyn Monroe. 他和玛明莲·梦露演对手戏。

out

(1) *used to indicate movement or direction from the inside to outside of something* 用来表示从某物的内部到外部的运动或方向。例如:

He went *out* the door. 他走出门。

She run *out* the door. 她跑出了门外。

He fell *out* the window. 他从窗口掉下来。

He was caught in the act of climbing *out* the window.

他在爬出窗外时被捉住。

(2) *used to indicate location* 用来表示位置。例如:

Out this door is the garage. 门外就是车库。

(3) *used to indicate movement away from a central point* 用来表示从中心点离开。

例如:

Let's drive *out* the old parkway. 让我们从老风景区干道驶出。

注: out 作介词用在英式英语中被视为非标准用语或非正式用语，要求用 out of, 但 out 作为介词用在美式英语中很普遍。

out of

(1) *from within to the outside of* 表示从里向外。例如：

The millionaire got *out of* the car. 这位百万富翁从车里出来。

She walked about in her room and then looked *out of* the window.

她在房间里踱来踱去，然后向窗外眺望。

注：上句中的 out of，在美式英语中常省略 of。

(2) *from*; *at a specific distance from* 摆脱；距离… 例如：

They did what they could to help her *out of* the difficulties.

他们尽其所能地帮助她摆脱困境。

The small village is about ten miles *out of* the mountainous town.

这个小村庄离山城约 10 英里。

(3) *from an origin, a source, or a cause* 表示起源、来源或原因。例如：

Many useful things can be made *out of* waste materials.

许多有用的东西可以用废材料做成。

She paid for it *out of* her salary. 她从自己的薪水里付了那笔钱。

(4) *from, as a motive or reason* 为了；由于。例如：

He did it *out of* curiosity. 他出于好奇做了这件事。

I say this *out of* kindness. 我出于好意这样说。

(5) *in a position or situation beyond the range, boundaries, limits, or sphere of* 表示超越界限、疆界、限制或范围的位置或情形。例如：

The plane flew *out of* sight. 飞机飞得看不见了。

This work is *out of* my reach. 这项工作是我能力所不及的。

(6) *in a state or position away from the expected or usual* 表示出乎意料的或不寻常的状态或位置。例如：

He was *out of* temper at this. 他听到这事发了脾气。

He was *out of* touch with his family during the war.

战争期间他与家人失去了联系。

(7) *from among* 表示"从…中"。例如：

Two *out of* ten households in cities now have computers.

现在城市里每十个家庭中就有两个拥有计算机。

You may choose *out of* them the one you like best.

你可以从它们中选择你最喜欢的一个。

(8) *in or into a condition of no longer having* 表示不再处于或进入拥有…的状态。例如:

Our car was *out of* gasoline on our way to the city.

在去该城市的途中我们的汽车没油了。

The situation there was *out of* hand. 那里的局势失去了控制。

We were tricked *out of* our savings. 我们的积蓄被骗走了。

(9) *used to express the negative result brought about by some action* 使…不，使…取消。例如:

We talked him *out of* doing it again. 我们劝说他不要再做这事了。

outside

(1) *on or to the outer or external side of* 在…外，位于或在…的外面或外侧。例如:

No pupil is allowed to stay *outside* the school during the school hours.

上课期间学生不得离校外出。

In the night she saw someone *outside* the window. 夜里她看见窗外有人。

(2) *beyond the limits of* 超出…的界限，如法律。例如:

No one is allowed to make fortune *outside* the law. 不允许任何人非法致富。

Modern abstract art is *outside* my province. 我对现代抽象艺术是外行。

(3) *with the exception of; except* 除了…；除了…之外。例如:

We have no other information *outside* the figures already given.

除了已提供的这些数字外，我们没有其他信息。

No one knows where he is *outside* his wife.

除了他妻子，没有人知道他在什么地方。

注: outside 的本义是"在外边"，引申为"超出范围"的意思，由此转用于表示"除外"。但这是口语、俗话的用法，在较正式的文字中不宜使用，而以用 except 为妥。

over

(1) *in or at a position above or higher than* 高于…；在…的上方，比…高。例如:

The lamp hung *over* the table. 那盏灯悬挂在桌子上方。

We must go *over* the mountain. 我们必须越过那座山。

The sun shone *over* our heads. 太阳在我们头顶上照耀。

注：over 与 under 正相反。例如：

> There was a sign *over* the door. 那门的上方有个标记。
>
> We saw a hawk gliding *over* the hills. 我们看见一只鹰在山顶上空滑翔。

(2) *above and across from one end or side to the other* 从一边或一端至…的另一边或另一端的上面，或越过上面。例如：

The dog jumped *over* the fence. 那条狗跳过篱笆。

The ball rolled *over* the grass. 球滚过草地。

(3) *to the other side of; across* 到…的另一边；越过。例如：

The old man strolled *over* the bridge. 那老人漫步过了桥。

(4) *across the edge of and down* 越过…的边缘向下。例如：

The man and his horse fell *over* the cliff. 那人和马从峭壁上摔了下去。

(5) *on the other side of* 在…对面；在…另一边。例如：

There is a village *over* the border. 边界对面有一个村庄。

(6) *upon the surface of* 在…表面。例如：

She put a coat of varnish *over* the woodwork. 她在木制品上涂了一层清漆。

(7) *on top of or down upon* 在…顶端上，在…的上部或落在…上。例如：

He tripped *over* the toys. 他被玩具绊倒了。

(8) *through the extent of; all through* 在…的范围内；遍及。例如：

She looked *over* the report. 她浏览了那份报告。

(9) *through the medium of; via* 通过…的媒介；经由。例如：

The president addressed us *over* the loudspeaker.

校长通过扩音器向我们发表了演讲。

I heard the news *over* the radio. 我从收音机上听到了这个消息。

(10) *so as to cover* 用于覆盖。例如：

She threw a shawl *over* her shoulders. 她把围巾披在她的肩膀上。

(11) *up to or higher than the level or height of* 达到或高于…的标准或高度。例如：

The water was *over* my shoulders. 水漫过了我的肩膀。

(12) *through the period or duration of; until or beyond the end of* 在…整个时期或期间；直到或超过…的结束。例如：

She has been working hard *over* the years. 这些年来她一直努力工作。

Are you staying *over* Christmas? 你打算留下过圣诞节吗?

(13) *more than in degree, quantity, or extent* 在程度、数量或范围上超过。例如:

At present the world population is *over* six billion.

当前世界人口超过六十亿。

(14) *in superiority to* 优先于。例如:

She won a narrow victory *over* her rival. 她险胜对手。

(15) *in preference to* 宁愿。例如:

We selected him *over* all the others. 我们比起别人更愿选择他。

(16) *in a position to rule or control* 处于统治或控制地位。例如:

No country can rule *over* the world. 任何国家都不能统治整个世界。

The director presides *over* the meeting. 该董事主持了会议。

There is no one *over* him in the department. 在这个部门没有人比他职位高。

(17) *so as to have an effect or influence on*; *on account of* 以便对…产生效果或影响; 原因。例如:

We all mourned *over* the death of the seven astronauts on the space shuttle—Columbia.

我们都在哀悼在哥伦比亚号航天飞机上死去的七名宇航员。

(18) *while occupied with or engaged in* (一面)忙于…(一面), 从事。例如:

We chatted *over* the tea. 我们边品茗边闲谈。

(19) *with reference to*; *concerning* 涉及; 关于。例如:

The couple often quarrel *over* trifles. 那两口子经常为小事吵嘴。

pace

with all due respect to; *with the permission of*; *with deference to, used to express polite or ironically polite disagreement* 蒙…恩准; 怀着对…的敬意得到允许; 顺从, 用来表示礼貌或讽刺性的礼貌的异议。例如:

I have not, *pace* my detractors, entered into any secret negotiations.

我没有, 请恕我无礼, 我没有参加任何秘密商谈。

I do not, *pace* my rival, hold with the ideas of the reactionists.

请允许我说, 我不赞成反动分子的意见。

past

(1) *beyond in time; later than or after* (在时间上) 超过；比…晚；在某个时间之后。例如：

He came back *past* midnight. 他半夜以后才回来。

It is *past* four o'clock. 已经过四点了。

Her mother is *past* eighty years of age. 她母亲已过八十岁。

(2) *beyond in position; farther than* 在位置上超过；比…远。例如：

The house is about a mile *past* the first stoplight.
这座房子在第一个交通指示灯大约一英里以外的地方。

The people walked *past* the memorial in silence. 人们静静地走过纪念碑。

The post-office is *past* the shops. 过去那些商店就是邮局。

注：上句中的 past，与 beyond 意思相同，可以互用。

(3) *beyond the power, scope, extent, or influence of* 超出…的权力、范围、程度或影响力。例如：

The problem is *past* the point of resolution. 这个问题实在无法解决。

The car is *past* repair. 这辆汽车已不能修理了。

(4) *beyond in development or appropriateness* 在进展或适宜程度方面超出。例如：

The child is *past* drinking from a bottle. 这个小孩已不再用奶瓶喝水了。

(5) *beyond the number or amount of* 在数目或数量方面超过。例如：

The child couldn't count *past* 30. 这个孩子数不到 30。

His ability is *past* compare. 他的能力是无与伦比的。

pending

pend 意为 "悬而未决，待决；吊着"，由于其现在分词位于名词之前而被视为介词，含义是：while in the process of; during 在…过程中；在…期间；while awaiting; until 在等待…之际；直到…为止。例如：

pending the negotiations 谈判期间

The money must remain in the hands of the trustees, *pending* a judicial ruling on the matter. 这笔款必须保持在托管人手中，直到此事司法裁决时为止。

This matter must wait *pending* her return from London.

这件事必须等到她从伦敦回来后再处理。

Pending his return, let us get everything ready.

让我们在他回来之前把一切准备就绪。

She was held in custody *pending* trial. 她被拘留候审。

Pending resolution of this matter, we ask you to hold all further shipment.

在此事尚未解决之前，我们要求贵方停止所有其他货物的装运。

per

（1）for each, *for every*, 每，每一。例如：

Gasoline once cost 40 cents *per* gallon. 汽油曾卖到每加仑 40 美分。

The vessel tax of anchorage is 5000 dollars *per* year.

这艘船的停泊税一年是五千美元。

Public houses are licensed to sell alcoholic drinks for a certain number of hours *per* week. 酒店持有酒类经销许可证，每周可按一定时数出售。

（2）*according to*; *in accordance with* 根据；依照。例如：

per the terms of the contract 按照法律条款

Changes were made to the manuscript *per* the author's instructions.

根据作者的指示，手稿做了改动。

The work has been donc as *per* instructions. 工作已按照指示做完。

（3）*by means of*; *by the agency of*; *by*; *through* 通过；用；借助于；经由，以…方式；通过。例如：

He sent the letter *per* his brother. 他那封信是由他弟弟寄出的。

注：❶ per 系拉丁语介词，主见于技术文章或统计学中，如: miles *per* gallon 每加仑英里数，work-hours *per* week 每周工作时数，feet *per* second 每秒英尺数。亦常用于体育评论。例如：

In the Olympic aerials event, each skier performs two jumps *per* round. After the first round, the first 12 move to the final round.

在奥运会空中特技滑雪赛中，每位选手每轮可以跳两次，第一轮比赛的前 12 名进入决赛。

在商务用法中，作"每，每一；根据，按照"解。例如：

Our offer is RMB300 *per* set of tape-recorder, F.O.B. Tianjin.

我们的报价是每台收录机 300 元人民币，天津离岸价。

在普通英语中用 a 或 an，在文学写作中不常用。

❷ 常见的短语有：

per your instructions 根据你的指示；

per annum 每年；

per capita 每人，按人，按人口；按人口计算；按人头分配；

per centum 每一百；

per contra 反之，相反；

per diem 每日；

per mensem 每月；

per mille 每一千；

per se 本身；本质上；

as *per* 按照；

as *per* usual 照常；一如既往。

plus

（1）*more by the addition of, increased by* 通过附加…增加，加上，加。例如：

Two *plus* two is four. 二加二等于四。

He had wealth *plus* fame. 他有钱又有名。

This work requires intelligence *plus* experience.

这项工作需要才智和经验。

Their strength *plus* their spirit makes them formidable.

他们的力量再加上勇气使他们难于战胜。

Intelligence *plus* wit makes for an interesting person.

智慧加上机智就利于造就一个有趣的人。

The construction slowdown *plus* the bad weather has made for a weak

market. 建筑的减少和糟糕的天气使市场疲软。

（2）*added to*; *along with* 加上；附加。例如：

a good job, *plus* a new car 一份好工作，附加一辆新车

ten pounds a week *plus* commission 每周 10 英镑附加佣金

The bill was $10, *plus* $1 for postage. 账款是 10 美元，再加上一美元邮费。

In the Dallas case, the employer had contracted with his employees for a

definite salary base per week, *plus* a bonus, *plus* overtime if earned.

在达拉斯一案中，雇主与雇员签约，明确每周薪水基数，加上奖金，加上如果挣得的加班费。

pro

pro 可作名词、形容词、副词，偶作介词，*for, in favor of* 同意，赞成。例如：

Are you *pro* capital punishment? 你赞成死刑吗？

He is generally *pro* new ideas. 他总是赞成新思想。

He is *pro* exercise but against physical exertion, quite a conundrum.

他赞成锻炼，但反对体力劳累，真是个难题。

qua

源自拉丁语单数阴性词 qui 的离格，in the capacity or character of; as 以…的资格或身份；作为。例如：

The President *qua* head of the party mediated the dispute.

总统以党的领袖身份出面调解这场争端。

Qua father, he pitied the young man; *qua* judge, he condemned him.

作为人之父，他同情那个年轻人；作为法官，他将他定罪。

He did it not *qua* father, but qua judge.

他不是用父亲身份而是用法官身份处理此事的。

Money, *qua* money, cannot provide happiness.

钱本身不能给人快乐。

He stated the opinion as a private person, and not *qua* president.

他以个人身份而不以总统身份表示意见。

re

in reference to; *in the case of*; *concerning* 就…而言；关于。源自拉丁语 in re，仅限于商业、法律文书，在一般语言文字里不宜使用。即使在商务通信中，re 的使用也常限于信函标题。例如：

re your esteemed favour of 1st inst 关于本月一日尊函

re your enquiry of the 19th October 关于您 10 月 19 日的询问

Re your question, the answer is as follows. 关于您的问题，答复如下。

We have not been informed *re* the mentioned price.

关于所提价格，我们尚未接获通知。

The case *re* the divorce will be heard on the 24th instant.

关于这桩离婚案将于本月 24 日开庭审理。

I want to talk you *re* the proposed meeting.

我想就被提议的会议同你商讨一下。

regarding

in reference to; *with respect to*; *concerning* 关于；至于；就…而论。例如：

I wrote a letter *regarding* my daughter's school examinations.

我写了一封关于我女儿学校考试的信。

Some good news *regarding* lung cancer had come a few months before.

几个月前传来了一些有关肺癌的好消息。

She said nothing *regarding* your request. 她对你的要求只字不提。

There is an article in the newspaper *regarding* the future of China's football.

报纸上登了一篇关于中国足球未来的文章。

注：参见 concerning 注释。

respecting

with respect to; *in view of* 关于；鉴于。例如：

Allow us to thank you for the fairness with which you have met us *respecting* this claim. 关于这项索赔，承蒙惠予公正处理，谨在此深表谢意。

We had quite a long discussion *respecting* the course to be adopted.

我们就有关将要采取的方针进行了相当长的讨论。

Respecting these facts, a special committee is to be appointed.

鉴于这些事实，必须成立一个专门委员会。

I am at a loss *respecting* the child's whereabouts.

关于孩子的下落，我茫然不知。

注：参见 concerning 注释。

round

（1）*so as to encircle or enclose* 围绕，环绕；围绕在。例如：

The earth goes *round* the sun. 地球围绕太阳转。

The children stood *round* the teacher. 孩子们围着老师站着。

(2) *at or to points on the circumference of* 到处，向…各处；在…四面八方。
例如：

On the eve of the lunar new year, we sat *round* the table eating and chatting away. 除夕之夜我们围坐在桌旁，不停地吃着，闲谈着。

She had a look *round* the shop. 她在店里各处看看。

(3) *having so passed* 转弯；绕过；附近。例如：

The grand hotel is *round* the corner. 那家大旅馆在拐角的地方。

He disappeared *round* the corner. 他转过拐角处就不见了。

Cheer up! Victory is just *round* the corner. 加油！胜利就在眼前。

The Mid-autumn Festival is just *round* the corner. 中秋节即将来临。

注：在美式英语中，上面的句子中 round the corner 写成 around the corner。

(4) *about; from beginning to end*（指时间、地点）大约；从…开始到末了。
例如：

They arrived *round* 7 o'clock. 他们大约七点抵达。

Verdant olives flourish *round* the year. 翠绿的橄榄树四季茂盛。

(5) *so as to make a turn or partial circuit about, or to reach the other side of* 迂回；绕道。例如：

An ocean-going vessel is coming *round* the cape.

一艘远洋货轮正在绕过海角驶过来。

sans

源自法语，用于古体和诗歌，*without*, 没有，无。例如：

sans hat and coat 无帽无外套

a bird *sans* feathers 一只没有羽毛的鸟

That ends this strange eventful history,

Is second childishness and mere oblivion,

Sans teeth, *sans* eyes, *sans* taste, *sans* everything.

终结着这段古怪多事历史的最后一场，

是孩提时代的再现，全然的遗忘，

没有牙齿，没有眼睛，没有口味，没有一切。

—Shakespeare's As You Like It, 1600

save

    with the exception of; *except*, 除⋯之外；除了。作为介词，该词现在在普通英语口语和书面语中已经过时，有时在诗歌和相当正式的文学体中仍然使用。save 与 except 同义，用于指对同类事物的排除，save for 与 except for 同义，则用来指对非同类事物的排除。in, but, except, save, besides + that 构成复合连词，表示"除⋯之外；只是；若非"之意。例如：

All is lost *save* honor. 除荣誉外一切都丧失了。

The parking lot was virtually empty *save for* a few cars clustered to one side. 除了几辆小车成群地停在一边，停车场几乎是空的。

比较：
{
The screen was all dark *save for* one bright spot.
除了一个光点，屏幕上一片黑暗。
The classroom was empty *save for* two girls.
教室里只有两个女孩。
}

She was fortunate *in that* she had friends to help her.

她很幸运，有一些朋友帮助她。

The situation is rather complicated *in that* we have two managing directors.

由于我们有两位总经理，所以情况很复杂。

But that I saw it, I could not have believed it.

要不是亲眼目睹，我还不信呢。

I agree with you, *save that* you have got one fact wrong.

我同意你的意见，只是你把一个事实弄错了。

She is well *save that* she has a sore throat.

除了喉痛外她一切都好。

Besides that the teacher explained the theory, he gave the students a lot of examples. 教师不仅讲解了理论，而且给学生举了许多例子。

saving

    with the exception of; *with all due respect to or for* 除⋯以外；尽管对⋯给予应有的尊重；表示异议时，有"恕我直言，冒昧地说一句"之意。例如：

Nothing remains *saving* three ruins. 除了三处废墟，一切荡然无存。

Saving your presence, I don't think the suggestion is very sensible.

请恕我直言，我认为这个建议不太合情理。

Saving yourself, nobody thanked me. 除了你本人外，没有人感谢我。

since

continuously from, from a particular time in the past until now 自…以来一直。
表示从过去某时延伸到现在的一段时间，常与完成时、完成进行时连用。例如:

They have been friends *since* childhood. 他们从幼时起一直是好朋友。

There have been many changes *since* the war. 战争以来发生了许多变化。

He has lived here *since* 1978. 他从 1978 年以来一直住在这里。

I've only been wearing glasses *since* last year. 从去年起我才一直戴眼镜。

He had worked at the bank *since* 1945. 他从 1945 年起就在银行工作。

than

in relation to; *by comparison with* (usually followed by a pronoun in the objective case) 关于，就…而论；与…比较 (后常跟宾格代词)。用于 than whom, than which 两个词组及某些用不及物动词的句中。例如:

He is a person *than* whom I can imagine no one more courteous.
他是我所能想象的最有礼貌的人。

He is a writer *than* whom there is no finer. 他是一位无与伦比的优秀作家。

It's a measure *than* which there was nothing better. 再没有比这更好的计策了。

Mary is more beautiful *than* anyone else in her company.
在公司里玛丽比其他人都漂亮。

There are more *than* 5,000 adjectives in that dictionary.
那本词典中有 5000 多个形容词。

I have no other pens *than* this one. 除了这一支我没有别的笔了。

He has no friend other *than* you. 除你之外他没有别的朋友了。

A student is not necessarily inferior to his teacher, nor does a teacher necessarily be more virtuous and talented *than* his students.
弟子不必不如师，师不必贤于弟子。

through

(1) *in one side and out the opposite or another side of* 穿越，从一边进，从相反的或另一边出。例如：

The train is running *through* the tunnel among the mountains.

这列火车正在穿过群山间的隧道。

(2) *among or between; in the midst of* 在…之中或之间。例如：

She often takes a walk *through* the flowers. 她经常在花丛中散步。

(3) *by way of* 由，经过。例如：

The thief climbed in *through* the window and was caught on the spot.

小偷从窗户爬了进去，但被当场抓获。

(4) *by the means or agency of* 通过，用…途径或媒介。例如：

He bought the antique vase *through* a dealer.

他通过一个商人买到了这只古花瓶。

She succeeded *through* hard work. 她努力工作取得了成功。

(5) *into and out of the handling, care, processing, modification, or consideration of* 经过处理、照料、加工、修改或考虑。例如：

Her application went *through* our office.

她的申请送交到了我们办公室审议。

She is running the figures *through* the computer.

她正在用计算机处理这些数据。

Atoms are so tiny that they cannot be seen even *through* the most powerful microscope. 原子非常小，甚至用倍数最大的显微镜也看不见。

(6) *here and there in; around* 各处，到处；各地。例如：

This famous writer is on a tour *through* France.

这位著名的作家正在法国各地旅行。

(7) *from the beginning to the end of* 从头到尾，自始至终。例如：

On the eve of Christmas, young people usually stay up *through* the night.

圣诞节前夜，年轻人通常通宵不睡。

I could not dance, but I sat *through* the party.

我不会跳舞，但我耐着性子坐到了最后。

(8) *at or to the end of; done or finished with, especially successfully* 在或到最后；尤指成功完成。例如：

We were *through* the initial testing period. 我们通过了最初的测试阶段。

We are *through* school at five o'clock. 我们五点上完了课。

(9) *up to and including* 直到并包括。例如：

They are going to stay on the mountains from Monday *through* Friday.

他们打算在山上从星期一一直待到星期五。

注：上句中的 through 是美式英语，英式英语一般用 to 或 up to。它所指
的时间包括其宾语所表示的时间在内，即包括星期五在内。

(10) *past and without stopping for* 通过而不停下。例如：

The driver was fined because he drove *through* a red light.

这个驾驶员因闯红灯而受到罚款。

(11) *because of*; *on account of* 由于；因为。例如：

The mistake was made *through* his fault. 由于他的过失造成了这个错误。

注：through 表示的原因，一般指偶然、意外等消极的原因。

throughout

(1) *in or to every part of*; *everywhere in* 遍及，到处，贯穿。例如：

They searched *throughout* the house. 他们搜遍了整个房子。

The disease spread *throughout* the country. 这种疾病蔓延到了全国。

Riot police are being deployed *throughout* the city to prevent any trouble.

防暴警察正在全城部署以防止动乱。

(2) *from the beginning to the end of*, *all through* 从头到尾；自始至终。例如：

It snowed *throughout* the night. 雪彻夜未停。

Australia were ahead *throughout* the game.

澳大利亚队在整个比赛中一直领先。

The doctors battled *throughout* the night to save her life.

医生们彻夜拼搏以挽救她的生命。

Throughout Europe a new railway age, that of the high-speed train, has
dawned. 在整个欧洲，一个铁路新时代——高速火车的时代，已经开始。

The temperature remained below freezing point *throughout* the day.

气温整天都保持在冰点以下。

His respiration grew fainter *throughout* the day.

一天下来他的呼吸越来越弱。

till/until

(1) *up to the time of* 直到…的时候。例如：

We danced *until* dawn. 我们跳舞跳到天亮。

(2) *before* (a specified time) 在 (某一特定的时间) 以前。例如：

People do not know the value of health *till* they lose it.

直到失去健康，人们才知道健康的可贵。

He didn't return *till* ten o'clock. 他到十点才回来。

She can't leave *until* Friday. 星期五之前她不能离开。

注：❶ 无论用作介词或连词，till 比 until 普通，在正式文字里多用 until；但这两个词所表达的意义是相同的，都表示"直到某时"。例如：

The people next door play their radio from morning *till* night.

邻居从早到晚开着收音机。

Stir with a metal spoon *until* the sugar has dissolved.

用金属勺子搅动直到糖溶解为止。

I slept *until* midnight. 我一直睡到半夜。

I didn't wake up *until* I heard the alarm clock.

直到听到闹钟的铃声我才醒来。

❷ 尽管这两个词所表达的意义是相同的，但应注意以下几点：

① until 和 till 两者都可作介词、连词，一般情况下可以互换使用。用于肯定句时，主句的动词只用延续性的，它所表示的动作一直延续到 till 或 until 表示的时间为止，意为"直到…为止"；用于否定句时，主句的动词一般是非延续性的，也可以是延续性的，它所表示的动作直到 till 或 until 所表示的时间才发生，意为"直到…(才)"。例如：

She didn't arrive *until* 6 o'clock. 她直到 6 点才到。

Don't get off the bus *until* it has stopped. 公共汽车停稳后再下车。

The EC will not lift its sanctions *until* that country makes political changes.

直到那个国家进行了政治变革之后，欧洲共同体才会取消制裁。

She watched TV *until/till* her mother came back.

她看电视直到她母亲回来。

（看电视的动作延续到母亲回来才结束）

She didn't watch TV *until/till* her mother came back.

直到母亲回来她才（开始）看电视。

（看电视的动作直到她母亲回来才发生）

② 当主句是肯定句时，它引出的意思是"直到（某时某动作停止了）"。例如：

The students made much noise *till* the teacher came into the classroom. 直到老师走进教室，学生们才停止了大声喧哗。

The young couple were very happy *until* they used up all their money. 那对年轻夫妇直到花光了所有的钱才沮丧起来。

③ 另外，until 可以放在句首而 till 则不可。

Until they used up all their money, the young couple were very happy.（正）

Till they used up all their money, the young couple were very happy.（误）

④ 否定句可用另外两种句式表示：

  a. Not until…在句首，主句用倒装语序。例如：

  Not until the early years of the 19th century did man know what hcat is. 直到 19 世纪初，人类才知道热能是什么。

  Not until I began to work *did* I realize how much time I had wasted. 直到我开始工作，我才认识到我已浪费了多少时间。

  Not until we pointed out his fault to him did he realize it. 直到我们向他指出了他的过错，他才意识到。

  b. It is/was not until…that… 直到……才。例如：

  It was not until 1911 *that* the first of the vitamins was identified. 直到 1911 年，第一种维生素才鉴别出来。

⑤ 此外，与较短的词组或从句连用时，多用 till。例如：

I shan't get back *till* late at night. 夜深以后我才能回来。

He had been in Beijing *till* last week. 他在北京一直待到上星期。

Wait *till* I call you. 等着我叫你。

⑥ 与较长的词组或从句连用时，多用 until。例如：

We didn't reach the station *until* after the train had left.

直到火车离开后我们才到达火车站。

She didn't come *until* late in the evening. 她直到晚上很晚才来。

⑦ 当它们引导时间状语从句时，往往要用一般现在时代替一般将来时。**例如**：

He will wait for you *until/till* your mother comes.

他将等你直到你母亲来。

⑧ 在强调句型中，not until 置于句首构成倒装句以及 until 放在句首时，均不能用 till 代替 until。**例如**：

It was *not until* 1920 that regular radio broadcast began.

直到 1920 年才开始有定期的无线电广播。

Not *until* 12 o'clock last night did Tom come back. （倒装句）

昨晚直到十二点汤姆才回来。

⑨ till 和 until 指时间，不指空间；如下面第一、二句正确，第三句不对：

The traffic laws don't take effect *until* the end of the year.

这些交通法规到年底才生效。（指时间）（正）

He walked *till/until* he reached the end of the street. （时间状语从句）（正）

He walked *till/until* the end of the street.（街的尽头，非时间）（误）

times

multiplied by 被乘以…。**例如**：

Two *times* four is eight. 2 乘以 4 等于 8。

Work is measured in terms of distance and force. Distance *times* force equals work. 功的计量是依据距离和力，即功等于力乘以距离。

The thermal conductivity of metals is as much as several *times* that of glass.
金属的导电率是玻璃的很多倍。

The earth is 49 *times* the size of the moon. 地球是月球的 49 倍大。

In this workshop the output of July was 4.5 *times* that of January.

这个车间 7 月的产量是 1 月的 4.5 倍。

to

(1) *in a direction toward so as to reach* 为了到达⋯而朝一个方向。例如:

The mayor intended to get *to* the bottom of the matter.

市长打算将此事追查到底。

He got *to* the station by five. 他五点前到达了车站。

(2) *towards* 朝着。例如:

Turning *to* the right, I entered a narrow path.

我向右转走进了一条狭窄的小路。

(3) *reaching as far as* 直到。例如:

The ocean water was clear all the way *to* the bottom.

海水从上面一直到海底都是清澈的。

(4) *to the extent or degree of* 达到⋯的范围或程度。例如:

She loved him *to* distraction. 她如此爱他, 以至于心神不宁。

(5) *with the resultant condition of* 以⋯为最后结果。例如:

He nursed her back *to* health. 他精心地照顾她, 使她恢复了健康。

They fought *to* the last drop of their blood. 他们与敌人血战到底。

(6) *toward a given state* 朝向某一状态。例如:

The government helped the minority women *to* economic equality.

政府帮助少数民族妇女取得了经济上的平等权利。

(7) *in contact with*; *against* 与⋯接触; 靠着⋯。例如:

Her face pressed *to* the windows. 她的脸贴着窗户。

(8) *in front of* 在⋯的面前。例如:

They stood face *to* face. 他们面对面地站着。

(9) *used to indicate appropriation or possession* 用于表示归属或占有。例如:

He looked for the top *to* the jar. 他寻找这个罐子的盖子。

This is the key *to* the door. 这是门的钥匙。

(10) *about, on, concerning* 关于; 至于。例如:

I am waiting for an answer *to* my letter. 我正在等回复。

(11) *in a particular relationship with* 与⋯有某种特定关系。例如:

The brook runs parallel *to* the road. 这条小河与路平行。

（12）*as an accompaniment or a complement of* 作为…的伴随或补充。例如：

She danced *to* the piano. 她和着钢琴跳舞。

（13）*composing; constituting* 组成；构成。例如：

two cups *to* a pint 两杯一品脱

（14）*in accord with* 与…一致。例如：

She took the job responsibilities suited *to* her abilities.

她担当了与她的能力相一致的工作。

（15）*in comparison with* 与…相比。例如：

This computer is superior *to* that one in performance.

这台计算机在性能上比那台好。

（16）*before* 差，在…之前。例如：

The time is ten *to* five. 现在是五点差十分。

（17）*up till; until* 一直到；直到。例如：

They work from nine o'clock in the morning *to* five o'clock in the afternoon.

他们从上午九点工作到下午五点。

（18）*for the purpose of* 为了…的目的。例如：

Will you please stay *to* dinner? 请你留下来吃饭好吗？

He has no title *to* our esteem. 他没有资格受到我们的尊敬。

（19）*in honor of* 向…表示敬意。例如：

Now I'd like *to* propose a toast to the health of the guests.

现在我提议为来宾们的健康干杯。

The Monument *to* the People's Heroes stands on the Tiananmen Square.

人民英雄纪念碑矗立在天安门广场上。

（20）*used to indicate the relationship of a verb with its complement* 用于指明动词和它的补语之间的关系。例如：

It is not necessary to refer *to* a dictionary whenever you come across a new word. You may guess its meaning from the context.

每当你遇到生词时，不必要查字典，可以根据上下文猜出其意思。

（21）*used with a reflexive pronoun to indicate exclusivity or separateness* 与反身代词连用，意为"独占或分离"。例如：

She has the room *to* herself. 她独占那个房间。

(22) *used to indicate ratio or proportion* 用来表示比率或比例。例如：

He proportioned the expenses *to* the receipts. 他量入为出。

(23) *used to denote attribution* 用来表示附属、归因。例如：

He owes his success *to* hard work and good opportunity.

他把成功归功于努力奋斗和良机。

(24) *used to connect adjectives, nouns, and intransitive or passive verbs with a following noun which limits their action or application* 连接形容词、名词、不及物动词或被动语态的动词和随在其后面用以限定动作或应用的名词。例如：

He yielded *to* me in this point. 在这一点上他向我屈服了。

He is endeared *to* his friends. 他为朋友们所喜爱。

Old memories constantly recurred *to* me. 往事经常浮现在我的脑海。

下列形容词后常接介词 to。

① 表示"行为表现"意义的形容词，如：kind, polite, courteous, merciful, cruel, impartial 等。例如：

She is impartial *to* her students. 她对学生一视同仁。

② 表示"品质、涵养"意义的形容词，如：loyal, true, faithful, false, just 等。例如：

He is faithful *to* his word. 他信守诺言。

③ 表示"有利、有害"意义的形容词，如：profitable, beneficial, hurtful, fatal, harmful, adverse, cross, detrimental 等。例如：

Lack of sleep is detrimental *to* one's health. 睡眠不足有害健康。

④ 表示"感觉、触觉"意义的形容词，如：sensitive, awake, alive, deaf, blind 等。例如：

He is deaf *to* all advice. 他对一切忠告置若罔闻。

⑤ 在某些主语和宾语易位的形容词之后，如：dear, hateful, detestable, abominate 等。例如：

The Huangshan Mountain is dear *to* me. 我爱黄山。

⑥ 表示"必需、重要"意义的形容词，如：essential, necessary, indispensable, useful, important, vital 等；或表示"难易"等意义的形容词，如：difficult, easy, possible, troublesome, tiresome, burdensome 等。例如：

Writing is easy *to* you (＝ It is easy for you to write).

写作对你来说很容易。

Health is essential *to* happiness. 健康是幸福必不可少的。

比较:
> Sleep is necessary *to* health.
>
> (睡眠对健康是必要的。)
>
> It is not necessary *for* you to go to school on Sundays.
>
> (星期日你没必要去上学。)
>
> I have everything necessary *for* the purpose.
>
> (我有这个计划所需要的一切。)
>
> Smoking is by no means necessary *to/for* me.
>
> (对我来说，抽烟根本没有必要。)

注: to 和 for 均可表示 "对…(来说)"，以下几点需注意:

❶ 在 necessary, good, easy, difficult, hard, impossible, suited, suitable, pleasant 等形容词之后，两者均可用。例如:

Food is necessary *to/for* us all. 食物对我们大家都是必要的。

但在形容词之后如接动词不定式时，通常用介词 for 来引出该动词不定式的逻辑主语。例如:

It's very hard *for* her to drive a bus.

对她来说驾驶公共汽车很辛苦。

有时形容词之后接介词 for，可认为是其后省略了一个动词不定式。例如:

This poet is too difficult *for* me (to understand).

这首诗对我来说太难(理解)了。

❷ 两者表示 "对…来说"，其区别是: to 通常只表示一般意义的 "对…来说"，即其意义较泛; 而 for 却含有比较、限制、区别的意味，它不仅表示 "对…来说"，而且含有 "限于…来说" 或 "只有对…来说" 的意味。例如:

English prepositions are difficult *to* almost all Chinese teachers and students of English, but they are not so difficult *for* my sister.

英语介词对于中国几乎所有学英语的教师和学生来说都是很难的，但对于我姐姐来说并不算难。

The lioness is ugly *to* all of us, but she is a beauty *for* the lion.

在我们大家看来母狮是很难看的，但对雄狮来说她却很美。

另外，有时两者的区别与主观和客观有关，即 to 强调主观，for 强调客观。例如：

It was a useful lesson *to/for* him.

这对他来说是一个有益的教训。

句中若用 to，表示"他"（him）自己认为有用（即主观）；若用 for 则表示写这句话的人（the writer）认为有用（即客观）。

⑦ 表示"起因"意义的形容词，如：due, assignable（可分配的，可归属的，可指定的），ascribable（可归于…的，起因于…的）等。例如：

Her success was due *to* perseverance. 她的成功是由于坚持不懈。

⑧ 表示"酬谢、责任"意义的形容词，如：grateful, thankful, responsible, answerable 等。例如：

I am grateful *to* you for your valuable help. 感谢你的鼎力帮助。

I am answerable *to* the company for the use of this equipment.

我要向公司承担使用这一设备的责任。

touching

(*literary*) *concerning; about, as regards*（文学用语）关于；涉及；提到。例如：

touching the subject of our conversation 有关我们谈话的主题

He wrote *touching* future plans. 他写了有关未来的计划。

Touching the budget considerations, we have several methods of saving money.

关于预算要考虑的事项，我们有几种省钱的办法。

注：参见 concerning 注释。

toward (s)

(1) *in the direction of* 朝着…的方向。例如：

He hurried *toward* (*s*) home after work. 下班后他匆忙往家赶。

(2) *in a position facing* 处于面对…的位置。例如：

She sat there silently with her back *toward* (*s*) the window.

她静静地坐在那里，背对着窗户。

(3) *somewhat before in time* 将近，在时间上比…稍前。例如：

It began to rain *toward* (*s*) morning. 快到早晨的时候，天开始下雨了。

He is verging *toward* (*s*) eighty. 他快八十岁了。

注：toward 和 towards 意思相同，toward 是古体，可互用。英式英语多
用 towards, 在美式英语多用 toward。

(4) *with regard to*; *in relation to* 关于…；和…有关。例如：

I take an optimistic attitude *toward* (s) the future. 我对未来抱乐观态度。

(5) *in furtherance or partial fulfillment of* 进一步促进或部分完成。例如：

He contributed five dollars *toward* (s) the bill. 他又还了五美元的债务。

(6) *by way of achieving*; *with a view to* 达到；以…为目的。例如：

Great efforts *toward* (s) peace will pay off.

为了和平所做的巨大努力将会成功。

(7) *of help to* 有助于。例如：

The mastery of a foreign language is an important step *toward* (s) obtaining
modern science and technology.

掌握外语是有利于获得现代科学技术的一个重要手段。

(8) *about, nearly* 大约，差不多。例如：

The plane rose *toward* (s) 10，000 meters above the ground.

飞机上升到离地面约一万米的高空。

under

(1) *in a lower position or place than* 在…下面，在比…低的位置或地方。例如：
The workers are digging a tunnel *under* the river.

工人们正在这条河的下面开掘一条隧道。

(2) *passing below or beneath something* 经过…的下面。例如：
The boat is passing *under* the bridge. 小舟正在从桥下通过。

(3) *to or into a lower position or place than* 到或进入比…低的位置或地方。
例如：

The boy rolled the ball *under* the couch. 男孩把球滚到了躺椅下。

(4) *beneath the surface of* 在…表面下。例如：

In the northwest, people make use of the water *under* the ground.

在西北，人们利用地下水。

(5) *beneath the assumed surface or guise of* 在…的假定表面或掩饰下。例如：

The novel was published *under* his pen name.

那部小说是用他的笔名出版的。

I declined his request *under* the pretence of inexperience.

我在没有经验的借口下谢绝了他的请求。

(6) *less than*; *smaller than* 少于，小于。例如：

The jar's capacity is *under* three quarts. 这个坛子的容量小于三夸脱。

(7) *less than the required amount or degree of* 未达到或少于规定之数量或程度。
例如：

Children *under* the age of 10 years are not allowed in.

10 岁以下儿童不准入内。

My shirt cost *under* two pounds. 我的衬衫价钱不到两英镑。

(8) *inferior to in status or rank* 地位或等级低于⋯。例如：

There were five officers *under* me at the headquarters.

总部有五个职位低于我的军官。

(9) *subject to the authority, rule, or control of* 在⋯的权威、统治或控制之下。
例如：

The small country is *under* a dictatorship. 那个小国受独裁统治。

(10) *subject to the supervision, instruction, or influence of* 在⋯指导下，受⋯
的监督、指导或影响。例如：

She made a big progress in playing the piano *under* her parental guidance.

在她父母的指导下，她在演奏钢琴方面取得了很大的进步。

(11) *undergoing or receiving the effects of* 经受或接受⋯的影响。例如：

The great old writer is *under* constant care.

这位伟大的老作家在接受长期护理。

(12) *bound or constrained legally or morally* 在法律或道德的强制或约束下。
例如：

He was *under* necessity to do that work. 他是被迫做那个工作的。

(13) *subject to the restraint or obligation of* 受到⋯的约束或承受⋯的义务。
例如：

Under article 3 of the agreement, the cease-fire order will come into force at
7 p.m. 根据协议第三条规定，停火命令将于下午七时生效。

(14) *within the group or classification of* 属于⋯的群体或类别。例如：

Tigers, lions, and jaguars come *under* the classification of the feline family.

老虎、狮子和美洲虎都属于猫科。

(15) *in the process of* 在…过程中。例如:

The ancient pagoda is *under* repair. 这座古塔正在维修中。

The economic scandal is *under* investigation. 这桩经济丑闻正在调查中。

(16) *in view of; because of* 考虑到…；因为…。例如:

Under any circumstances a gentleman has no right to hurt a woman.

在任何情况下，绅士都无权伤害女士。

(17) *with the authorization of* 经…的授权。例如:

The armored division is *under* orders for the front.

这个装甲师正在奉命开赴前线。

(18) *sowed or planted with* 播种或栽种着…。例如:

She has five acres *under* wheat and rape. 她种了五英亩的小麦和油菜。

(19) powered or propelled by 以…为动力，或用…推动。例如:

Locomotives *under* steam are no longer in use.

以蒸汽为动力的火车头已不再使用了。

underneath

(1) *below the surface or level of; directly or vertically beneath; at or on the bottom of* 在…表面或平面之下；直接或垂直地在…之下；在…的底部。例如:

The coin rolled *underneath* the piano. 硬币滚到钢琴的下面了。

Soot gathers *underneath* the boiler. 烟灰积聚在锅炉底下。

She sat *underneath* the tree in the shade. 她坐在树阴下。

The baby liked to sit *underneath* the table. 这婴儿喜欢坐在桌子底下。

(2) *under the power of; under the control of* 在…权力范围内；在…控制下。例如:

Underneath the department heads are the junior executives.

这些部门首脑下面是下级的经理主管人员。

(3) *hidden, disguised, as by a false appearance or pretense* 在虚假外表或虚伪掩盖、伪装之下。例如:

Underneath his bluster is a timid nature. 他的咆哮下是胆小的本性。

Underneath his ingratiating manner, I felt a sinister intention.

在他阿谀的态度底下，我感到一种阴险的意图。

注: 当讨论物质东西和空间关系时，在英语口语和一般书面中，underneath 比 beneath 普通得多，但 underneath 不可以用于表示非物质的和非空间的意义，用于比喻义除外。例如:

Underneath his apparent politeness there was deceit and cunning.

他谦虚的表面下掩盖着欺骗和诡诈。

unlike

(1) *different from*; *not like* 不同于；不像。例如:

She's *unlike* the rest of her family. 她不同于她家里的其他成员。

Her latest novel is quite *unlike* her earlier works.

她最近的小说与她以前的作品截然不同。

A person, *unlike* a machine, is not replaceable.

人和机器不同，人是不可替代的。

Unlike his brother, he has a good sense of humor.

和他兄弟不同，他很有幽默感。

(2) *not typical or characteristic of* 非…的特征的或典型的。例如:

It's *unlike* him not to call. 不打电话过来对他来说是不多见的。

It's very *unlike* him to be so abrupt. 这么粗鲁可不像他平时的样子。

It is *unlike* her to enjoy herself so much. 过得这么开心不像她平时的样子。

unto

(1) *to* 对，给，于。例如:

He spoke *unto* her. 他对她说。

Do *unto* him as he does *unto* others. 以其人之道，还治其人之身。

Peace be *unto* you. 愿平安降临于你身上。

He is a law *unto* himself. 他是个一意孤行的人。

Be faithful to husband *unto* death. 从一而终。

Smooth is the way that leads *unto* wickedness. 通往邪恶的路是平坦的。

Do not *unto* others what you wish not done *unto* you. 己所不欲，勿施于人。

(2) *until* 直到。例如:

a fast *unto* death 一直坚持到死的斋戒

The soldier was faithful *unto* death. 这位战士至死忠贞不渝。

(3) *by* 在…旁边。例如：

a place *unto* itself, quite unlike its surroundings

一处幽静的地方，与其周围的环境大不一样

注：与 until 第一成分同源，18 世纪以来，主见于典雅、古风或圣经文体中。

up

(1) *from a lower point to or toward a higher point on* 朝高处，从一个较低的地点走到或走向更高的一点。例如：

We began to go *up* the mountain at daybreak. 拂晓时我们开始上山。

He went steadily *up* the social scale. 他在稳步地爬社会的阶梯。

(2) *toward or at a point farther along* 朝向或位于更远的某个位置。例如：

The car stopped at two miles *up* the road.

小汽车在路前方两英里处停了下来。

(3) *toward the source or head of a river or lake* 向河流、湖泊等的上游，溯…而上。例如：

The ship is sailing *up* the river. 这艘船正在扬帆溯江而上。

She lives *up* the street. 她住在街的那边。

(4) *toward or into the interior of country* 向或进入内地。例如：

Many new factories have been built *up* the country.

这个国家建起了许多新工厂。

(5) against 与…相反。例如：

The plane was flying *up* the wind. 飞机当时正顶风飞行。

upon

(1) 同 *on*。例如：

The village stands *upon* a hill. 这个村庄座落在一座小山上。

Upon (= *On*) his arrival at the airport, the man was arrested by the police.

那男子一到机场就被警方拘捕了。

(2) on 和 upon 的用法比较：

① upon 与 on 意义相同，但语气较为正式，在口语中多用 on。upon 只用作介词，on 既可作介词又可作副词。

② 表示日期, 习惯用 on, 而不可用 upon。

③ 少数成语中习惯用 upon 而不用 on, 如 *upon* my word (决不食言), *upon* this (于是), once *upon* a time (从前, 有一次) 等。

④ 在句末一般用 upon。例如:

This report is to be depended *upon*. 这份报告是可靠的。

⑤ 作 "紧接着" 或 "逼近" 解时, 用 upon 而不用 on。例如:

The enemy was *upon* us. 敌人在逼近我们。

The Christmas holiday will soon be *upon* us. 圣诞节马上就要到了。

versus

(1) *against* 反对。例如:

the plaintiff *versus* the defendant 原告对被告

restriction *versus* opposition to restriction 限制与反限制

That's a matter of outs *versus* ins. 那是在野党人与执政党人的对抗。

(2) *as the alternative to or in contrast with* 与…相反或与…相对。例如:

freedom of information *versus* invasion of privacy 信息自由与抄袭侵权相对

traveling by plane *versus* traveling by train 坐飞机旅行与坐火车旅行比较

We should choose peace *versus* war. 我们应该选择和平, 反对战争。

注: versus 作介词主要用于法律与体育中, 常缩写为 vs. 或 v.。

via

(1) *by way of* 经过, 经由, 取道。例如:

We went to Pittsburgh *via* Philadelphia. 我们经过费城到匹兹堡。

This flight is routed to Chicago *via* New York.

这班飞机是经纽约飞往芝加哥的。

He flew to Europe *via* the North Pole. 他经由北极飞到欧洲。

(2) *by means of* 通过, 凭借。例如:

to send the letter *via* airmail 通过航空邮寄信件

a solution *via* an inquiry 通过调查解决

I can send him a note *via* the internal mail system.

我可以通过内部通信系统给他发个通知。

vice

instead of, in place of, as a substitute for 代替，接替。源自拉丁语 *vix* 的离格，*vicis* = change，作 "改变，替换，代替" 解。例如:

He became chief accountant *vice* John, who had resigned.

他代替已辞职的约翰，成为主会计师。

John Doe was appointed postmaster *vice* Richard Roe retired.

约翰·多伊被任命为邮政局长，取代退休的理查德·罗。

I will preside over the meeting, *vice* the absent chairman.

我将代替缺席主席主持会议。

vis-a-vis

in relation to; *compared with*; *facing*; *opposite* 关于；与…比较；与…相对。例如:

They were now *vis-à-vis* the most famous painting in the Louvre.

他们这时面对着罗浮宫内最著名的绘画。

This year's crop shows an improvement *vis-à-vis* last year's.

与去年相比，今年收成有所增加。

His salary *vis-à-vis* the national average is extremely high.

他的薪水比起全国平均水平高出很多。

The U.S. position *vis-à-vis* the major developed regions deteriorated as well.

美国对主要发达地区的地位也衰弱了。

Because of the considerable appreciation of the yen *vis-à-vis* other currencies in this period, however, the actual cost of Japanese goods in foreign markets rose more rapidly than those of many other nations.

然而，由于这一时期日元对其他货币有了相当大的升值，与许多其他国家相比，日本货物在外国市场上的实际成本上升得更迅速。

wanting

(1) *lacking*; *without* 缺；没有。例如:

a letter *wanting* a stamp 一封没有贴邮票的信

a box *wanting* a lid 一个没有盖子的盒子

a book *wanting* a cover 一本没有封面的书

(2) *minus*; *less* 差；少。例如：

an hour *wanting* 15 minutes 差 15 分钟一小时

a century *wanting* three years 差 3 年一个世纪

Wanting common sense, a man can do nothing well.

一个人缺乏常识，什么事也干不好。

Wanting mutual trust, friendship is impossible.

缺乏彼此信任，就谈不上友谊。

Wanting courage, nothing can be done. 缺了勇气，什么都办不成。

with

(1) *in the company of* 在…陪伴下。例如：

Will you go to the movies *with* me? 你陪我一起去看电影好吗？

(2) *next to*; *alongside of* 在…旁边，同…在一起。例如：

She sat *with* her family chatting. 她和家人坐在一块儿聊天。

(3) *having as a possession, an attribute, or a characteristic* 带来或具有某属性或特点。例如：

They arrived *with* glad tidings. 他们带来了喜讯。

He is a man *with* a moustache. 他是个留着小胡子的男人。

(4) *used as a functional word to indicate accompanying detail or condition* 用作功能词，表示伴随的细节或状况。例如：

He just sat there *with* his mouth open. 他只张着嘴坐在那儿。

With her permission, he left. 获得她的允许后，他离开了。

I escaped *with* just a few bruises. 我逃跑时只受了一些擦伤。

(5) *in a manner characterized by* 以…方式，多与抽象名词连用。例如：

She performed *with* great skill. 她技巧娴熟地表演着。

We listened to her *with* interest. 我们饶有兴趣地听她讲述着。

(6) *in the charge* 负责，照料。例如：

She left the cat *with* the neighbors. 她把那只猫托邻居照管。

(7) *in support of*; *on the side of* 支持，赞同。例如：

He is *with* us on that issue. 在那个问题上他支持我们的观点。

(8) *in the same group or mixture as*; *among* 把…混在同一组或混合物中；在…之中。例如：

He planted onions *with* the carrots. 他把胡萝卜和洋葱种在一起。

(9) *in the membership or employment of*; *working for* 是…的成员，为…工作或服务。例如：

She is *with* a publishing company. 她受雇于一家出版公司。

注：上句中的 with 是美式英语用法，意为 "working for, serving under 为…工作，在…之下服务"。

(10) *by the means or agency of*; *by the use of* 用通过…的方式或媒介；用…工具，可接具体名词或抽象名词。例如：

She eats *with* a knife and fork. 她用刀叉吃饭。

He made us laugh *with* his jokes. 他用笑话逗我们笑。

This is a pillow stuffed *with* feathers. 这是一个充满羽毛的枕头。

(11) *in spite of* 尽管，通常与 all 连用，与 for all 同义。例如：

With all her experience, she could not get a job.

尽管很有经验，她还是找不到工作。

(12) *in the same direction as* 以…相同的方向。例如：

Our ship sailed *with* the wind. 我们的轮船顺风起帆。

(13) *at the same time as* 与…同时。例如：

The old lady usually gets up *with* the birds. 这位老太太通常与鸟儿同时起床。

(14) *in regard to* 关于，对于。例如：

She is pleased *with* the new apartment. 她对新公寓很满意。

(15) *in comparison or contrast to* 与…相比；与…对照。例如：

My opinion is identical *with* his. 我的意见和他的意见相同。

(16) *and*; *plus* 和；加上。例如：

My books, *with* my brother's, make a sizable library.

我的书加上弟弟的书就成了一个相当大的图书馆。

We had turkey *with* all the trimmings. 我们吃了加各种调料的火鸡。

(17) *inclusive of*; *including* 包括。例如：

The total sum comes to $29.95 *with* postage and handling.

包括邮资和手续费总金额为 29.95 美元。

（18）*in opposition to*; *against* 反对；对抗。例如：

He was wrestling *with* an opponent. 他正在和对手摔跤。

（19）*as a result or consequence of*; *because of* 由于…的结果或后果，因为，多表示一种生理或心理状况的原因。例如：

She was trembling *with* fear. 她吓得发抖。

He was sick *with* the flu. 他患了流感。

比较：
$\begin{cases} \text{She wept \textit{at} the bad news.} \\ \text{She wept \textit{over/for} the death of her child.} \\ \text{She wept \textit{for/over} the deceased (dead).} \\ \text{She wept \textit{with/for} joy.} \end{cases}$

注: to weep at 见 / 听了…而哭泣，指由于外界事物的刺激而使感情有所波动的原因；to weep over 仅指感情产生于某一事变上；to weep for 表示同情的行为表现；to weep with 表示心理上的极端反应，由刺激而产生的一种行为状态。

（20）*so as to be touching or joined to* 加入，联合为了取得联系；把…连起来。例如：

They coupled the first car *with* the second.

他们把第一辆汽车和第二辆配成双。

（21）*so as to be free of or separated from* 离开，脱离，与…分离。例如：

I parted *with* her after many years. 多年后我和她分手了。

（22）*in the course of* 在…的过程中。例如：

One does not grow wiser *with* one's age.

人并不随着年龄增长而变得更有智慧。

（23）*used as a functional word to indicate close association* 用作功能词，表示密切联系。例如：

With the advent of cheaper and more powerful personal computers in the 1980s, use of CAI increased dramatically.

随着20世纪80年代价格更便宜、功能更强大的个人计算机的出现，计算机辅助教学的应用显著地增加了。

（24）with＋宾语＋宾语补足语构成的复合结构在句中主要作状语，表示伴随、原因、时间、条件、方式等；其中的宾语补足语可以是名词、形容词、副词、现在分词、过去分词、不定式、介词短语等。

① with ＋宾语＋名词

She used to sit reading in the evening *with her pet dog her only companion.* 她从前常在晚上坐着看书，她的宠物狗便是她唯一的伙伴。

He died *with his daughter yet a schoolgirl.* 他去世时，他的女儿还是个小学生。

② with ＋宾语＋形容词

I like to sleep *with the windows open.* 我喜欢开着窗户睡觉。

She came into the room, *with her nose red* because of cold.

她走进了房间，鼻子冻得通红。

③ with ＋宾语＋副词

He fell asleep *with the light on.* 他睡着了，灯还亮着。

The boy stood there *with his head down.* 这男孩低着头站在那儿。

④ with ＋宾语＋介词短语

He was asleep *with his head on his arms.* 他把头枕在手臂上睡着了。

She said good-bye *with tears in her eyes.* 她含着眼泪说了声再见。

The soldier had him stand *with his back to his father.*

士兵让他背朝着他的父亲站在那儿。

⑤ with ＋宾语＋现在分词

指动作正在进行或在当时看来已是一种在持续的状态。例如：

With spring coming on, trees turn green. 春天到了，树变绿了。

The little girl called out to her mother, *with tears running down her cheeks.* 小女孩大声呼喊着她的母亲，眼泪顺着脸颊流下来。

With prices going up so fast, we can't afford luxuries.

由于物价上涨很快，我们买不起高档商品。

注：正如进行时态有时可以表示将来意义一样，有时现在分词也可表示将来意义。例如：

With winter coming on, it's time to buy warm clothes.

冬天就要到了，该买暖和衣裳了。

⑥ with ＋宾语＋过去分词

指与其前的名词或代词为被动关系。例如：

He sat in the chair *with his legs crossed.* 他盘着双腿坐在椅子上。

She had to walk home *with her bike stolen.*

她的自行车被偷了，她只好步行回家。

⑦ with ＋宾语＋动词不定式

通常表示不定式所表示的动作尚未发生或在当时看来尚未发生。

例如:

The kid feels excited *with so many places of interest to visit.*

有这么多的名胜可参观，小朋友很激动。

With no one to talk to, John felt miserable.

由于没有可以说话的人，约翰感到很悲哀。

I can't go out *with all these clothes to wash.*

要洗这些衣服，我不出去了。

within

(1) *in the inner part*; *inside* 在⋯里面，在⋯内部。例如:

Solidarity must be strengthened *within* and without the Party.

必须在党内外加强团结。

By the use of X-rays, doctors can see *within* the body.

医生用 X 光可以看到人体内部。

(2) *inside the limits or extent of in time or distance* 在时间或距离的限度或范围之内。例如:

The bus stop is *within* 100 meters of the railway station.

公共汽车站离火车站不到 100 米。

He will complete the dictionary *within* half a year.

他将在半年内完成这本字典。

(3) *inside the fixed limits of*; *not beyond* 在固定的限制之内；不超出。例如:

She lives *within* her income. 她量入为出。

My house is *within* walking distance of my university.

我家离我的大学很近，走过去就行了。

(4) *in the scope or sphere of* 在⋯范围内；在⋯领域内。例如:

Any business must act *within* the law. 任何商业必须在法律允许范围内活动。

There have been tremendous advances *within* the medical profession.

医学专业领域已经出现了巨大进展。

(5) *inside a specified amount or degree* 在确定的数量或程度内。例如：

I can only afford to buy the encyclopedia *within* 100 dollars.

在 100 美元以内我才能买得起这部百科全书。

(6) *in the mind of* 在…心中。例如：

I feel *within* me that I can manage it. 我觉得我能应付得了。

without

(1) *not having*; *lacking* 没有；缺少。例如：

The day passed *without* accident. 这一天平安无事。

(2) *not accompanied by*; *in the absence of* 没有陪伴；没有…。例如：

Without a moment's hesitation, she jumped into the river to save the drowning girl. 她毫不犹豫地跳进河里去救溺水的女孩。

Please don't leave *without* me. 请让我和你一起去。

(3) *at, on, to, or toward the outside or exterior of* 在外面；对着外面；向着外部。例如：

Why do you remain standing *without* the door? 你为什么仍站在门外？

(4) *not lacking* 通常与 not, never, cannot 等否定词连用，构成双重否定，表示语势很强的肯定。例如：

There are almost no families *without* televisions in cities.

现在城市里没有电视机的家庭几乎没有了 (现在城市家庭几乎都有电视机)。

One cannot learn English well *without* constant practice.

没有不断地实践，我们是不可能学好英语的。

(5) without 复合结构

和 with 一样，介词 without 也可以带宾语＋宾语补足语构成复合结构，宾语补足语可以由形容词、副词、介词短语、现在分词、过去分词、动词不定式 (及其短语)、动名词充当，在句中主要作状语，表示时间、原因、条件、方式、结果以及伴随情况等。

① without ＋宾语＋现在分词

Possibly this person died *without anyone knowing where the coins were hidden*. 这个人死去时，可能没有任何人知道那些钱币的隐藏地。

I'm so mad at him; he left *without anybody knowing*.

我对他十分恼火，没有任何人知道他就离开了。

② without＋宾语＋过去分词

The conference hurriedly finished *without a single agreement reached.*

会议仓促地结束了，没达成任何一个协议。

The battle was over, *without a shot being fired.* 一枪未发，战斗就结束了。

③ without＋宾语＋动词不定式

It was a poor village, *without machinery to do any of the work.*

这是个贫穷的村子，没有机械干农活。

It was boring to sit there *without anything to do.*

无所事事地坐在那里太无聊了。

④ without＋宾语＋介词短语

Yesterday I saw him belting through the fourth ring road *without any thought to the other motorists.*

昨天我看到他在四环路上飞驶，全然不顾路上其他开汽车的人。

I don't like sweet coffee; I like it better *without sugar in it.*

我不喜欢加糖的咖啡，里面不加糖我更喜欢。

⑤ without＋宾语＋副词

I'd be lost *without you here.* 没有你在这儿，我一筹莫展。

Without the network on, no information could be gained from Internet.

网络不通，就不可能从网上得到任何信息。

⑥ without＋宾语＋动名词

Words change meaning *without our noticing.*

不经意间，词汇的意义已经发生了变化。

They debated for hours *without a decision being taken.*

他们争论了几小时，也没作出决定。

⑦ without＋宾语＋形容词

The volume of air varies directly as temperature, *without pressure changeful.* 在压力不变的情况下，空气体积与温度成正比。

worth

(1) *of a value equivalent to* 相当于…价值；值…钱。例如：

The vase is *worth* 500 dollars. 这花瓶值 500 美元。

I paid only £ 300 for this used car, but it's *worth* much more.

买这辆旧汽车我只花了 300 英镑，但它的价值要高得多。

(2) *deserving of*; *meriting* 值得的；应得的。 例如：

Knowledge is *worth* working for. 知识是值得努力追求的。

That place is definitely *worth* visiting. 那地方无疑值得一游。

(3) *having wealth or riches amounting to* 具有达到…的财富或财产。 例如：

She is *worth* a million pounds. 她有一百万英镑的财产。

注：《牛津袖珍英汉双解词典》(*Pocket Oxford English-Chinese Dictionary*) 将 worth 标为表语形容词，用法像介词；而兰登书屋的韦伯斯特美 国英语词典 Random House Webster's Dictionary of American English 则标为介词。

英语学习
案头工具书

**English
Reference Book**

《英语单词词根词缀记忆法：看这本就够》

简 介：精心选取了常见的词根前缀和后缀，配上例词拆解和例句，直观展示单词结构，并给出拓展词汇，你想记不住都难。

《英语常用短语大全集(第2版)》

简 介：本书精选日常生活中常见的短语，剔除了那些比较生僻的内容，在一定程度上减轻了学习者的负担，而且更具有针对性。

《实用英语红宝书:语法活用大全》

简 介：一本超全的英语语法归纳总结书！新思维，新学法，用23个典型语法知识，总结语法精髓。搭配更多常用的例句，活学活用词法、句法。

《实用英语蓝宝书:介词用法大全》

简 介：一本超全的英语介词归纳总结书！小介词，大用法，教你分清楚！附赠2000道介词练习题，用介词夯实英语基础。

《实用英语绿宝书：同义词近义词辨析》

简 介：一本超全的英语近义词使用总结书！一个意思，多种表达，细微差别决定成败，超600组词语辨析让语言输出更丰富、更准确。

《新工程制图英汉—汉英两用词典》

简 介：本书是一部涵盖了多专业工程制图的英、汉互译工具书。它不仅是一部词汇，而且是一部对有关标准名词、易混淆词、新词、难词，都给了精要注释，为读者提供查阅研究的专业词典。

《英语构词法大全》

简 介：本书共分为六章，收录了632个词根，83个前缀，189个后缀。对每个词根、前缀和后缀的来源、含义都做了考证和阐释，有的还做了分析区别。

《18000英语单词分类速记口袋书》

简 介：本书是一本内容覆盖相当全面的单词书，囊括了生活中常见的15个主题，每个主题下又细分了多场景，全书共有426个场景。生活中方方面面的单词几乎都可以在这里找到。开本精巧，适合随身携带。